RURAL MINISTRY

RURAL MINISTRY

The Shape of the Renewal to Come

Shannon Jung
Pegge Boehm
Deborah Cronin
Gary Farley
C. Dean Freudenberger
Judith Bortner Heffernan
Sandra LaBlanc
Edward L. Queen II
David C. Ruesink

ABINGDON PRESS
Nashville

RURAL MINISTRY
THE SHAPE OF THE RENEWAL TO COME

Library of Congress Cataloging-in-Publication Data

Rural ministry : the shape of the renewal to come / Shannon Jung . . . [et al.].
    p.   cm.
    Includes index.
    ISBN 0-687-01606-1 (alk. paper)
    1. Rural churches—United States.   I. Jung, Shannon
1943.– .
    BV638.R87   1998
    253'.0973'091734—dc21   98-12313
                                                                        CIP

Unless otherwise noted, all scripture quotations are from The New Revised Standard Version Bible, copyright © 1989 by the Division of Christian Education of the National Council of the Churches of Christ in the USA. Used by permission.

Excerpts from *The Rural Ministry Primer* are used by permission.

98 99 00 01 02 03 04 05 06 07— 10 9 8 7 6 5 4 3 2

MANUFACTURED IN THE UNITED STATES OF AMERICA

To all the saints
who formed rural congregations
and communities into
models of Christian grace and service.

Among them:
unsung pastors, priests, and church workers;
farmers and ranchers,
shopkeepers,
doctors, nurses, and midwives;
leaders in the Town and Country Church Movement;
founders of the National Catholic Rural Life Conference and
their United Methodist, Baptist, Presbyterian,
Lutheran, UCC, Brethren, Mennonite,
and other Protestant compatriot organizations;
women religious;
schoolteachers and women's church auxiliary movements;
and rural advocacy groups.

CONTENTS

Congregational Life and Mission

PREFACE

Promising and challenging things are happening in rural ministry. We know. We are a team of nine who have worked together on many rural projects over the years. On this book we have struggled together in many ways; some of the most entrenched were over theology. So, Lutheran Sandy and Southern Baptist Gary went round and round on how to talk about the "kingdom of God." The team worked together on this project for better than three years. We represent Lutheran, Presbyterian, Roman Catholic, Southern Baptist, and United Methodist churches. All told our team has over 120 years experience in rural America—as pastors, as farmers, as directors of rural ministry centers, as denominational officials, as continuing education directors, as seminary teachers, and as foundation staff. We are opinionated; each of us holds firmly to our beliefs and appreciates our denominational traditions. We have worked together, however, and we firmly believe this book is stronger for that collaboration. We believe that the book symbolizes both our ecumenicity and the optimal future of rural ministry, namely the commitment to embodying a respectful, shared, cooperative, community-revitalizing ministry in the name of the living Christ.

Our purpose here is straightforward: We believe that God is calling rural churches to a new vision, a transformation of character that is evangelistic, missional, and deeply satisfying. Rural ministry confronts the central challenges of our era: the changing world economic order, the globalization and questionable sustainability of the world's food supply, the environmental crisis and controversies, racism and migration, equitable access to social and public services, and—most centrally—the question of how we can live together, community.

These are not simply social questions, they are questions addressed to the churches of Jesus Christ. They are congregational and theological questions. In short, the challenges of our time are deeply spiritual and will involve religious answers. God is calling rural parishes to be witnesses to the resurrection, to promote reconciliation between enemies, to care for the life of the world, and the salvation of our own souls and those of all others.

So this book invites you to a conversation—with rural church members, with priests and pastors in those churches, with seminarians, and with any who are concerned about community in America. We think that the church requires the best and the brightest in rural America, and that the rural church can lead the way.

Three Pressing Questions

The crisis that we are called to address, and which we invite the reader to ponder, raises three questions: "Why change?", "What are our options?", and "How can we move from where we are to where we think we ought to be?"

The first question, "Why change?", requires a reality check. The first section of this book will **describe the nature of the crisis** of rural people, rural community, and the health of the land. Clear analysis of the complex dynamics of the rural context is a prerequisite for creative change in the direction of more sustainable futures. We cannot be content with the social and economic situation, nor the spiritual condition in rural America today. The biblical view of what ought to be our relationship with all of God's creation calls us to a careful problem analysis.

Thus, the first part of the book is devoted to a well-crafted description of the rural context. Chapter One is an overview of the trip—not a summary, but an invitation. After considering the history of the churches' rural work in an effort to learn from past movements (Chapter Two), we explore the present context of rural America as described by Alvin and Heidi Toffler's "third wave" information age in Chapters Three and Four. We are well aware that this volume cannot be sensitive to the dimensions of every regional context and recommend that you search out additional resources specific to your ministry location. Chapter Five outlines the societal issues washing over rural America and confronting the church.

Understanding the nature of the crisis we face raises a second question and the issue of **vision**. "Do we have any options for a different future?" Do we have a Biblical and theological vision about a more promising future for the people, the land, and future generations? In what directions is the church called to lead? How are rural congregations already incorporating elements of that vision? Does this vision reflect our maturing historical perspectives about the impact of civilization upon the land?

Thus, the second section of this book is devoted to the issue of vision. In this section we ask several questions: "What Biblical resources inform this vision?" "In what directions is this vision pointing?" Chapter Six offers a contextual Biblical-theological foundation that is thematic and sensitive to local churches. The moral directions and principles that flow from our understanding of God's actions form the topic of Chapter Seven.

The third question that the rural crisis raises is about **strategy**. "*How* do we move from where we are to more holy, just, and sustainable futures?" The third section of the book looks at the challenging and strategic role of the church in the process of the renewal of the rural community and the land.

How might we re-vision the ministry of the church within the perplexing spiritual, social, economic, and political realities of contemporary rural America? It is important to realize from the beginning that the crisis we address challenges many of our historic assumptions. We will suggest some ways our faith communities, parish life, theological education, and lay ministries can respond to what is happening to rural communities.

The concluding section of the book offers a vision of the future of the rural church's work (Chapter Eight) and takes up rural congregational life to offer models of what is possible and also offers some practical, first steps for a future-oriented ministry (Chapter Nine).

Chapter Nine can serve as an example of the group's collaboration. Deborah Cronin wrote the first draft; it was critiqued by the whole group on a ranch in Missouri and in an airport hotel in the Twin Cities, over Mongolian foods and chocolate-covered peanuts. An editing subgroup meeting in Dubuque recognized the urgency of making the last chapter as practical and inclusive as possible. Thus we sought out friends to enrich our thinking. The subgroup then melded their suggestions and met again for the final edit. The Epilogue is similarly collaborative.

Consistently throughout the book we use "boxed text" to illustrate what is being talked about in the main body of the chapters. These tend to be stories about congregations or Biblical quotations or hymns or other materials that round out the text. We really like them and hope you will too.

Language sometimes proved to be a problem for us. For example, the Roman Catholic term for local church, "parish," was a bit strange for some Protestants; so also the Protestant equivalent, "congregation," was not familiar to Roman Catholics. We fought about whether to use "American" or "U.S." There were more than a few examples of different terminology, some gender-related, some denominational, some related to polity. Our policy has been to use all such terms and to ask readers to try to accommodate unfamiliar ones.

We are all still working and learning. This effort is the best we can offer you at the moment, but we hope that if you have suggestions for improvements or other stories or jokes or whatever you think ought to be taken into this account, you will send them to one of us.

There are usually quite a few people who deserve acknowledgment for assisting in the production of a book. Multiply that by nine and you see our dilemma. How could we possibly thank all those whose questions in the course of workshops, teaching, lecturing, and so forth have sharpened our thought and pushed us in more stimulating directions? It is clearly impossible. However, our collaboration itself honors those faithful Christians whose thought is represented here through us. This has been a delightfully and often hard-fought collaborative effort.

And so, being unable to name all who influenced this book, we must acknowledge only a few: the members of the Rural Church Network in North America, a group of seminary professors and denominational leaders engaged in rural ministry; the Reverend Jim Cushman; Dr. Mary Lee Daugherty; the Reverend Ed Kail; Brother David Andrews, C.S.C., Esq.; Dr. Bernie Evans; and Father Norm White. Thanks also to Claudia Krogmann, Kris Kirst, Anne Helmich, and Patty Walker who typed and coedited at the Center for Theology and Land. We also thank The Henry Luce Foundation for a grant undergirding our travels to argue with each other and form long-lasting friendships; our colleagues at the various organizations we serve; and—above all—our families who sustain the core of our Christian community and represent God's presence with us.

May God bless you in your ministry, whether on the tractor or in the kitchen, the pulpit or the podium, the office or the shop.

CHAPTER ONE

An Introduction to the Vision

As people of biblical faith, we write this book because we must. We are called to proclaim both the salvation wrought by Jesus Christ and God's vision for human flourishing. What we see happening in the rural sector of our society is the opposite of what the Bible says about how God wants us to live with the land, with all creation, and with each other. In the Bible we see that all creation is good and that all creatures and all parts of creation are important to God.[1] Human beings are created in the image of God and have responsibility to care for all of creation.[2] Keeping the land, having trusteeship of it, means accepting responsibility for the maintenance of justice and righteousness throughout our sphere of influence. God has made a covenant with humanity and with all creation.[3] Biblical wisdom invites us to live our lives in accordance with the divine plan and intention for creation.[4]

Furthermore, Christ gave his disciples and church a commission to minister to the needs of common people and to call all persons to a vital, life-changing faith in God. Sixty-one million of those people live in rural America—more than ever before. Rural communities are now much more diverse than is commonly believed. Farmers, frequently thought to be the largest segment of the rural population, are in fact fewer in number than at any time since the 1890s. A higher percentage of rural families live in poverty than urban families. Demographic changes are putting real pressure on the churches in rural America to respond to their needs. Consider the following example:

A Report from Rockville

Sharon came in to talk about what was happening in the rural community where she is a United Methodist student pastor.

"Can a community experience depression?" was her opening question. "It certainly seems like that's what's happening in Rockville. Last week there was a terrible car accident. The mother and two children in one car were killed; her husband, who was driving, is recovering. The woman in the other car is okay. But she is a teacher in town; he farms close to town; they are both members of Rockville Methodist.

"Last year a high school junior ran his car into a tree at high speed. Some people think it was a suicide. Anyway, now his whole class has dropped out of school activities. I talk to people in my congregation and some of them can tell me about tragedies that happened to people from Rockville year-by-year for the past twenty years. They even remember the names of all twenty."

In the course of our conversation Sharon shared what she had learned about Rockville. Even though the population of the town has not changed, the downtown area is now a row of empty storefronts. There are a couple of gas stations/convenience stores/restaurants on the highway, but the three grocery stores and in-town gas stations are gone. People drive forty-five minutes to shop in larger towns.

"Furthermore, the number of farms and farmers is down. People worry about pesticides but they feel like they don't have much choice about how to farm.

We still have the school—a plus—and we still have the churches. But the sense of powerlessness is deep."

Rockville seems to have experienced more than its share of tragedies; other than that, however, the story Sharon told is all-too-typical of many towns. The rural church is being called to respond to the forces that are affecting its community.

Sharon's last question was one that countless pastors and lay people are struggling with: "How can the church address this situation?"

The church's role in rural America (including Rockville) is understood as offering hope, proclaiming God's promises, and announcing salvation (Pss. 24, 33; Rom. 8). As disciples of Christ, we are called to follow in Jesus's footsteps in pursuit of his vision of God's community coming on earth as it is in heaven. This reign, or kingdom, is one of justice and righteousness tempered in love and forgiveness. As visionaries, we are concerned to make God's presence felt in Rockville—God's healing, God's hope for a healthier, more whole community. We witness to the salvation that God intends for us all and we work to make our prayer, "Thy kingdom come on earth, as it is in heaven," a reality. We stand in that hope. We are energized with a vision about a different future, God's future.

As laborers in the field of rural ministry, we conclude that the Rockvilles and countrysides of this nation are in crisis. Our society is not providing for the redemption of the land as called for in Lev. 25:24. Fields are being joined to fields so that nowhere can the people be found (Isa. 5:8); rural people are losing their neighbors. Houses (or business establishments) are being joined to houses, just as Isaiah observed in his time. Further, there are millions of persons who have not experienced God's grace by trusting in Jesus, and millions more who are not actively involved in the life of a local church. At least 40 percent of the people in rural America are unchurched, according to the Glenmary Research Center in Atlanta, Georgia.[5] There are many dimensions to the crisis. Yet, in crisis we recognize hope and opportunity. We observe that there is a need for change. In this recognition there is tremendous possibility. That is why we are energized. The need and possibility for

16

change are evident. Thus, we stand at the threshold of new opportunity.

Because of these new realities of crisis and hope, we write about the need for re-visioning and transforming the ministry and the mission of the church in rural America. The first section of this chapter will describe the nature of the rural situation that cries for change. The second part of the chapter lays out the biblical and theological foundations of rural congregations. Third, we turn to emerging, pioneering models. The church is a sleeping giant; it is engulfed in the rural crisis, but it also has God's salvation and purposes to proclaim. It is strategically positioned to initiate change in the direction of more promising futures for individuals, for human community, and for the land itself. The problem that we address is of historically unprecedented magnitude. This book tries to fathom its complexity so that we can more efficiently strive for renewal.

Why the Sense of Crisis?

What is at stake in all of these concerns? Why all the effort invested in the publication of a book on rural ministry?

What is at stake is nothing less than the salvation of persons, the health of the land itself, and the welfare of human communities—rural, urban, and suburban—both in this country and around the world. What is at stake is the salvation, the health, and welfare of future generations. At stake in the rural crisis is the question of social, interspecies, and transgenerational justice. These ever-growing dimensions of justice form the new frontiers of Western thought. They are anything but limited to the rural sector itself. They intersect with questions about the spiritual health of believers and nonbelievers in communities everywhere.

At stake in the rural crisis is the question of national and global food security and food safety in a world of declining per capita caloric food intake and a growing concern about toxicity in our food supply. Almost all high quality arable land is now under intense cultivation. Human populations continue to grow at unprecedented rates. On a global average, annual soil loss is now estimated at eleven tons per hectare.[6] The magnitude of the consequences resulting from these concerns places us in unexplored territory.

At stake in the American rural crisis is the issue of the stability of democratic society. By and large, decisions about what happens to the land and rural communities are being made outside the local community. The ideals of a participatory, self-determining society are threatened, particularly in the rural sector. The long-term trend toward delegitimatizing the federal government has been both the result and the cause of the rise of militias in rural areas;[7] there are other groups—racial and ethnic, income groups, lifestyle enclaves—that threaten and antagonize each other. The reality of new international trade agreements, with seats of arbitration located in distant lands, is illustrative of the forces that are currently eroding fundamental ideals about democratic life. The changes initiated by forces promoting massive welfare reform, decreased spending on social programs, and tax cuts are not promising for less affluent people anywhere. These changes also influence the spiritual health of rural Christians. Caught in this global rural crisis is the church. The stakes are high!

Is our present understanding about the life, work, and witness of the rural church adequate for the twenty-first century? Does its history provide a precedent for a new era? At Canberra, Australia, in February of 1991, the Protestant ecumenical world articulated the need for the renewal of the whole creation.[8] Recent papal writings point to the same need.[9] At Rio de Janeiro, the United Nations held its conference on environment and development where the idea of sustainable development was officially launched. The Kyoto Protocol of 1997 addresses global warming. In one way or another, the entire world, both secular and religious, is addressing the issue of planetary survival. Old assumptions about limits are giving way to new assumptions about responsibility. The familiar saying of

18

an Ohio farmer when speaking to his child about "leaving the place in better shape than when you took it over" has become a world-wide moral imperative in a world where short-term privatized profits frequently have more power and appeal than long-term benefits for the good of all.

We write this book in a moment of tremendous opportunity because the need for change from resource-exhausting practices to sustainable development is widely recognized. However, there is little clarity about how to make the transition from short-term profits to the flourishing of all life. We confess that a God's-eye-view is essential at this kairotic moment. That is the challenge.

The time is right for working toward new options for the rural sector of the society. The crisis we address is world-wide in magnitude. This book could be useful for churches in other nations, even though we focus on the role of the church in the rural U.S. We are writing about the need to re-vision the mission of Christ's church in this globally connected and bewildering rural context. We write about the need for re-visioning at a moment in time when leaders and decision-makers, who are largely urban-based, have too often lost touch with rural concerns. As an ecumenical team, we are working with a wider, more comprehensive and inclusive lens.

The thesis of this book is simple. The authors believe that the church in rural America today not only can, but must, contribute significantly to the renewal of individual people, the land, and the communities of people rooted in the land, as well as in urban places. In and underlying this renewal is the energy of the Spirit. The church will gain its life by rethinking what the commissions of Christ (Matt. 6 and 28) mean for the work of the contemporary rural church in America. It will gain its life by trusting God for its salvation and by actively working to define, develop, and implement a comprehensive and inclusive view of the good.

In view of all that has been said thus far, one might ask, "What is new in this book?" The authors believe that there are

19

three elements. The first is found in the analysis of the rural crisis that points to the inseparable relationships between rural communities, including their families and their churches, with public and corporate policies, science, technology, and industry, and the land. If we are to talk about the renewal of the whole creation and move ourselves onto a path of sustainable development, then we have to work for the renewal of all four inseparable elements of persons, community, economy, and environment.

Second, what is new in the book is our focus upon the mission of the local congregation or parish in the rural sector of society. We intend for our understanding of this spiritual mission to conform to the biblical call to renew the whole creation and the secular challenge of sustainable development. We are called to discover God's ways of living, to live in ways that are Spirit-sustaining, and also to assure that future generations will be able to meet their needs in a healthy way in communities all over the world.

Third, for years rural ministry has been placed on the back burner. We will contend that it must be in the forefront of the planning and work of the twenty-first century church. It is here that one will find great opportunity to formulate new models of congregational life that address emerging realities.

Biblical and Theological Foundations

Rural communities confront us with a paradox. In many rural parishes there seems to be little basis for hope, and yet Christian hope abounds. Perhaps this is a case where God's "power is made perfect in weakness" (2 Cor. 12:9). This section will first describe that paradox and then suggest where the foundations of that strange and wonderful hope lie. These are the building blocks of the vision of resurrection this book offers. The church is Christ's amazing instrument for creating life out of death.

20

The situation in many rural communities like Rockville is depressing.[10] The number of grocery stores, banks, hardware stores, doctors and nurses, and schools is smaller today than it was. It is discouraging for churches to see the pictures of large confirmation classes from twenty years ago when today's class has only two or three students. The young continue to leave some rural counties for metropolitan areas and the remaining rural populations tend to be older and poorer than the average in urban areas.

Why do rural people stay? Why not pack it in and move away? Why not sell the farm or, less drastically, take out the wind breaks, plant every square inch, and let the next person worry about erosion and chemical runoff? And the church—why do its members refuse to be shut down? Why do they cling to life when it would be "more efficient" to merge with the large church thirty miles away?

The future of rural communities is threatened, but so is the future of inner-city and even suburban communities. The question of sustainable development that we often associate with developing countries has become real in the United States. Though our concern here is with rural communities and rural ministry, it may well be that our vision also applies to a broader range of communities.

In numerous rural communities, the church is the most resilient institution. It is the "convenor of community," and out-survives even the local tavern! The church witnesses to a hope beyond decline; it remains realistically optimistic even in a depressing situation. It offers a vision that buoys the spirits of many rural peoples. It serves as a fellowship center and the base for many community initiatives. The church still strives to live out the spirit of love and grace in which it was founded. It sometimes comes close to being a place where "everyone knows my name," and cares about me and mine as I do about them and theirs.

What is the source of this hope? What does the Christian faith have to offer that seems to speak with such energy to rural

21

communities? How is it that churches remain such vital centers?

What Makes Them the Heart of Many Communities?

Let us suggest five reasons why the Christian faith has sustained communities with such dogged hope. These can also be seen as resources that the church has to offer rural people. We will revisit these themes in Chapter Six. They also form the basis of the vision that we perceive being born in rural America.

1.) The Christian faith empowers us to understand reality and to face those aspects of life that are painful. It describes the way life really is, even when that reality is changing rapidly, and includes suffering and loss. Central to that picture is our faith and hope in God.

The biblical witness indicates that the whole world, ourselves included, belongs to God. We do not control all of reality, nor does our final (or even immediate) happiness depend on how *we* perform. Through our hope in God's future we find the strength to face an unadulterated view of all of life, warts and sin as well as beauty and virtue.

Most forcefully making this point are those portions of Scripture having to do with creation. "The earth *is the Lord's* and all that is in it, the world, and those who live in it; for he has founded it on the seas, and established it on the rivers." (Ps. 24:1–2).

Throughout the entire witness of Scripture there is a strong emphasis on God's continuing involvement with the creatures—plants and animals, men and women. Scripture also presents reality as interconnected; each species has its particular role in the ongoing vibrancy of the planet. The Hebrew word *shalom* expresses the way God designed each part of the organism to depend upon other parts and to give support to yet others. The earth is intended as a cosmic unity; much of

22

that design is still visible. The world is a garden and God is the Master Gardener. Our partnership with the Master Gardener requires us to possess an inclusive, long-range vision of human community while never forgetting that the Master Gardener is in charge.

Much of the suffering and pain humankind experiences is self-inflicted. The capacity we gardening partners have to disrupt the design or to further it has also become greater. Human sinfulness leads citizens of affluent nations to overproduce, overconsume, and despoil the garden. Nor have we human beings adequately respected and cared for our companion gardeners. We have upset the balance of natural community and specific human communities.

We Christians believe that God "who is faithful and just will . . . cleanse us from all unrighteousness" (1 John 1:9). The world is permeated with the grandeur and providence of God. It is in the power of God's grace that we hope. The life, death, and resurrection of Jesus Christ definitively witness to our own deliverance from the powers of darkness. Finally, it is the sure and certain hope of the resurrection that makes many rural churches hopeful in the face of decline.

2.) The Christian faith also offers rural residents the possibility of a transformative community of care and work.

The church community, the body of Christ, burst into life by the power of the Holy Spirit at Pentecost (Acts 2). The descendants of that apostolic community claim the same promise of the Spirit that Jesus made to the original twelve that he would be with them always (Matt. 28:20). Christians have been saved from depending on their own inability to save themselves through a dependence on the Spirit. Ironically their own capacities have gained renewed power through being disposed rightly, toward God's purposes.

Jesus Christ left us this gift of the church, the community of the faithful; the local congregation is still the visible sign of God's grace. It is a community of people united by Christ in their faith and called to love one another.

The church is also a real community of people who are called to work together to help realize God's purposes. In a metaphor that reminds us of the *shalom* of creation, the church is portrayed as an organism which, when each part is working properly, makes for bodily growth in love (Eph. 4:15–26; 1 Cor. 12:12–31). Local churches work toward meeting the goal of doing Christ's work, being God's agents or deputies. They are strengthened by the celebration of the sacraments and the proclamation of the Word for life in this world.

The rural church is the place where the Christian vision for our lives meets the routine of the everyday, and can transform the everyday into vocation. This calls church members both to individual faith, to God-given daily work, and to corporate action. "Work in the church" carries over into our everyday vocations in the world. It is clear that working together in the church is a powerful witness to the presence of God. Furthermore, it increases people's hope and faith. We build each other up.

Living the Vision

Concerned about the on-going farm crisis, the Deer Creek Presbyterian Church of Camden, Indiana partnered with Faith Lutheran Church, a rural church three miles away, to begin the Church and Community Project. Determined to work on the problems of the aged, youth, and community development, the two churches incorporated into Active Care Develops Community, and together have pulled the community into many activities and programs which meet the existing needs of the community.

These activities include a 40+ Group to bring people over age 40 together. They sponsor the Deer Creek Festival, a yearly event with food and entertainment for community building. They have established a Beautify Deer Creek Area project to clean up and make absentee landlords responsible for their property.

> They have worked on developing a park out of an historic landmark at Sycamore. They sponsor a summer youth recreation program. They advocate for citizens to receive their share of government resources. They sponsor a Community Yard Sale to bring the community together and promote the area. They are working on developing a gathering place for community discussion and socializing. This effort is ongoing and plans to continue developing activities and programs to meet existing and emerging community needs.
>
> *Seeds in the Wind: Creative Models for Rural Ministries*
> **Evangelism and Development Unit, Presbyterian Church (USA)**

3.) Christianity offers individual men and women ways of finding meaning in their lives through the worship of God and faith in Jesus Christ.

Much of Scripture is directed toward the spiritual renewal of people's personal lives. If Christ is "the way, the truth, and the life" (John 14:6), then we are called to worship and find God's truth, and to live lives centered on Jesus Christ. We go to church to worship. But it is also important to pray individually.

Conceived as spiritual exercises, our private and quite personal devotions are directed toward listening and hearing God's word to us. Small groups of Christians worshiping together can combine private meditation on Scripture with sharing and listening. Combining private devotions with a time of thinking together with others about where God is moving in our own lives *and* in the lives of others frequently deepens our understanding of the movement of the Spirit. That spiritual sharing can lift a parish out of the depression that comes with no vision.

The impact of doing spiritual exercises upon our character and attitude formation is crucial. It enables us not to be crushed by death, suffering, and long-term communal decline but to be "transformed by the renewing of your minds" (Rom. 12:2). As significant as directions for corporate action are, we need also to attend to the individual sources of spiritual strength.

4.) Christians desire that family and neighbors come to share their faith in God and experience the fruits of the Spirit, and they pray and witness toward the goal of sharing their faith with others.

A shared faith in God can be the most effective base for just and loving community life. Even in the many communities where the church has taken the form of different theological and denominational expressions, there should be a shared core of beliefs that promotes unity within diversity. We all have sinned (Rom. 3:28) and need the redemption, grace, and forgiveness that Christ brings.

All Christian churches have the privilege of sharing the good news of God's love and salvation with others. Indeed, they cannot help but share that joy. They want others to experience the ultimate peace and purposefulness that accompanies that faith; they want others to know the results of life in the Spirit—joy, peace, patience, and kindness (Gal. 5:22). Finally, rural Christians want all others to share the truth of Jesus Christ and the vision of the kingdom that Jesus lived and proclaimed.

5.) Christians believe that God can help them discover moral directions for their own lives and the life of their community.

Our faith directs us to care for ourselves, for other human beings, and for the whole earth. We earlier used the metaphor of human beings as gardening partners with the Master Gardener. If the whole earth is a garden then we are all directed to tend the places where we are—those "places," let it be noted, include plants, men and women, animals, the land and waters, boys and girls, and also our own selves. We are to care for the world as God's home, which we share with all others.[11]

This directive to care becomes specific and personal in rural communities. What is the quality of life in this place, this town? What is God doing here now and how can I cooperate with God? How can I glorify God in the way I farm or mine or carry on business; how do I sustain land and community? What is the quality of the human community here; do people here experience the care and nurture appropriate to their full personhood? How is God present in people's spiritual lives; do they experience God's forgiveness; am I forgiving others? Do I live out God's forgiveness?

One way of assessing the direction in which rural communities are moving is to compare those directions with God's purposes. Would God endorse those directions? Another way is to ask "What will the quality of life and the health of the land be like in this community ten years from now if present trends continue? How does that projection compare with God's purposes?"

Finally, one aspect of God's meaning for our lives is to act in such a way that our worship of God can continue. We should work for an economy and a politics where the worship of God can flourish. This is a call to identify false gods and idolatrous moral directions. It is especially hard to do in a culture that often endorses values that are at variance with Christian concerns for the common good, the well-being of the disadvantaged, and the health of all creation. When short-term privatized profits and individual advantage are the ascendent values, the preservation of a society with the freedom to proclaim and live out Christian values is absolutely vital. Here the search for justice comes in close conversation with our spiritual exercises, our private and personal relationship with Jesus Christ.

In concluding this section, we remember that the church is the body that Christ entrusted to carry on his movement. Sometimes it is not hard to remember that we "have this treasure in clay jars" (2 Cor. 4:7)! Nevertheless, it *is* the treasure of God's activity among us. It is God's presence finally that accounts for the hope that we in the rural church have. That is the source of our hope! Figuring out how we are to carry out God's will requires the best of our ingenuity and Spirit-filled reflection. How can we best be the church of Jesus Christ in the rural community? That will be the focus of the third part of this book, and of the next section of this chapter.

Being the Church in Rural America

God created us in community, a community that lives on the land together with all living things. We are charged to care for this living community and to live within this community with God in whose image we are created, who is also our parent and our guide. When we are together in community as church, we are assured that we are all members of this body. The Holy Spirit was given to us at Pentecost to be with us, guide us, and inspire us. The Garden of Eden is long behind us, and we are left in the midst of a current situation in the rural community where as church, it is important to offer the hope that we can again find God, our image, our parent, and our guide. Discerning God's call in the midst of the turmoil and change in rural America is the challenge and opportunity that all who minister in rural America face.

In order to minister effectively in a rural setting, it is important to know the *congregational* identity; the ethnic, cultural, and/or theological roots as well as the history of the congregation; and the geography and the sociology of the place. In addition, it is important to understand the traditions of the other institutions in the *community*, the other denominations, and also the economic situation that exists in rural America as well as in the local community. Those who would do effective ministry in rural America need to understand and address the whole community. The needs and concerns of rural communities, rural churches, and rural life are profound.

The church in the United States is undergoing profound changes—mainline churches are no longer the single dominant church in the U.S.; evangelical churches are on the rise; denominational offices are downsizing; giving trends are down in mainline churches. In addition, the fact that evangelical churches are more conservative theologically and socially, while mainline churches are traditionally more liberal, causes another tension. But things are changing; mainline churches are thinking about evangelism; evangelical churches are addressing environmental and social needs. The downsizing of national, regional, and judicatory staffs with a subsequent decrease in services and programs creates another pressure on the rural church.[12]

The rural *congregation or parish* is undergoing changes that include yoking or pairing churches; merging or blending of churches from different denominations; the closing of parishes; and difficulty calling pastors to rural areas. At the same time *communities* are experiencing declining populations; more migrant workers; depressed local economies; environmental degradation; an increase of poverty among rural residents and an influx of urban poor into rural areas; and a rural population that has been significantly affected by a variety of governmental and corporate policies and by a tightening of funds for many public services, including education.

The interaction between the changes in society, in U.S. Christian denominations, in rural communities and rural churches is often played out locally and understood and articulated quite well by parishioners. An excellent example of this comes from Catholic participants in a two-year focus group research project sponsored by the National Catholic Rural Life Conference.

When participants were asked what needs of their rural communities should be addressed, their responses included the following:[13]

- economic issues—jobs, jobs, jobs (especially good quality, safe, well-paying jobs);
- social service needs;

- the need for human respect and acceptance of who rural people are;
- an acceptance (and availability) of mental health services;
- ways for churches to stay open and viable;
- a vision of a viable community;
- understanding how to address urban problems that are now appearing in rural settings (drug-dealing, gang activity, etc.) in addition to those that have historically been part of the rural scene;
- transportation and health care needs.

The list could go on. Participants talked at great length about the demands upon their time; school (especially sports) is becoming the center of community life; less often does the church serve in this capacity. In addition, the increasing amount of work time now required by family wage earners to provide for the necessities of life for their families has diminished the amount of time available for church and other community activities. People are more drawn into a family structure that has itself become more fragile as a result of the pressure on life in rural communities today.

The participants went on to outline what they considered the root causes of these rural problems. Some of the causes are: less population; the inadequate prices farmers are receiving; concentration of land and markets in the hands of a few; lack of a vision for a sustainable community; raising children to leave rural America rather than affirming a desire to stay; regulations; too much cultural homogeneity; individualism that runs counter to community; and often times a closed system (if you weren't born here, you don't belong).

The participants were asked about leadership for local churches. Their responses named the following needs:

- finding leaders who are not already over-committed;
- many families with two parents holding one or more jobs, each finding less time available for "church work";

- many people don't see themselves as leaders, because they don't think they're good enough;
- education is important because, if people are informed and confident, they can be leaders;
- the biggest obstacle to lay leadership is the ordained; and finally,
- many people do not want to step forward to be leaders because of the risk of criticism or recriminations.

What can the church do to respond to these needs? The focus group participants were quite clear in what they wanted. (You might want to consider how what they said could apply to the way the faith community in Rockville could address the situation that Pastor Sharon described at the beginning of this chapter.) The focus group noted, first, that it was important for churches to affirm rural life and help change attitudes of helplessness or inferiority. Members and officials should keep rural churches open and viable through proactive planning; one way of doing this is to integrate rural life into the liturgical and community life of the church. Churches could advocate for small businesses and the family farm structures and follow through with programs that will continue to serve rural people. They could provide a voice for rural people on regional, national, and international levels by working with like-minded organizations and developing collaborative relationships. Above all, however, they urged **the churches to become involved in church-based community building that will address systemic problems that occur in rural communities.**

Models of Rural Church

During the past decade, problems in the rural church have intensified; many people do not feel that the church is relevant to their lives or filling a need. It is important to identify the type of rural church that does meet the needs of the local community.[14] Many people are arguing that the church is changing and must continue to change. In the pages that follow we give examples of church-related models and also one or two secular models that are suggestive of future directions for the church. In all cases, communication is essential.

Peter Drucker, in his book, *The New Realities*, states:

> For communication to be effective there has to be both information and meaning. And meaning requires communion. If somebody whose language I do not speak calls me on the telephone, it doesn't help me at all that the connection is crystal clear. There is no 'meaning' unless I understand the language—the message the meteorologist understands perfectly is gibberish to a chemist. Communion, however, does not work well if the group is very large. It requires constant reaffirmation. It requires the ability to interpret. It requires a community.[15]

Rural communities in America can have a built-in advantage because of their size, if we use Drucker's hypothesis that communion "works" best in a small group where everyone understands the language. The language of rural communities must of necessity include the history of the community, the church, and the economy as well as the environment. Once the communication is understood, then it is possible to move on to communion and community. All three words have the same Latin root *communis*, which means "to hold in common."

The first model of church we would offer is that churches form coalitions to work out of a larger understanding of the needs of rural communities, as well as a larger understanding of the place of the church in today's society. No longer can we work in isolated units; the complexity of our society demands that we introduce the interrelated aspects of our world. Rural America as well as the rural church no longer can or should stand alone. We must adopt an independent worldview. We must consider that the current definition of church is changing.

As we look at an ecological worldview, it is important for churches in rural communities especially to understand that they must work in consort or in coalition with existing organizations within the community.

The word *coalition* comes from a Middle Eastern word that means merchants banding together for safety ... known as "companies" which literally meant "bread-sharers." How appropriate that this book is now calling for rural Americans in their rural ministry to come together to form coalitions or "bread-sharers"! We come together as bread-sharers in communion based upon **communication** and within **community**. We share in a real sense the living bread of Christ and we search out coalitions where we can also find the face of Christ in our midst. Matthew 25: 34-36 tells us exactly what we need to do:

> Then the king will say to those at his right hand, "Come, you that are blessed by my Father, inherit the kingdom prepared for you from the foundation of the world; for I was hungry and you gave me food, I was thirsty and you gave me something to drink, I was a stranger and you welcomed me, I was naked and you gave me clothing, I was sick and you took care of me, I was in prison and you visited me."

We have claimed that providing hope is an important role of the church. Throughout the United States, we can find models of church that provide hope for rural America and the rural church. These models of hope are impacting community in systemic ways that show signs of promise for years and perhaps generations to come.

One of the most theologically profound examples of work in the Midwest today is the Land Institute in Salina, Kansas. Here Wes Jackson, his interns, and staff are discovering native perennial crops that are suited to the environment. Jackson seeks to work in harmony with God and nature rather than assuming that human beings are mechanically in control of nature. This theological shift reflects a changing understanding of creation and human partnership with God's *shalom*. In addition, the Land Institute has a cafe that includes a menu outlining the different foods offered (primarily from the local community) and where they came from—an emphasis on community and the community's interdependent relationship, another aspect of *shalom*. Perhaps the Land Institute is a new model of fellowship (or even church) that provides hope for the future and for interdependence within the community.

Another model is the Congregation (or Community) Supported Agriculture projects (CSA's) throughout the U.S. As more urban dwellers become concerned about the safety of their food supply, they are looking to family farmers to supply fresh food and vegetables to them directly. One CSA located in the Rochester, New York, diocese has developed adult education programs that talk about the spirituality of creation; they connect food supply, agriculture, and world hunger; model outreach to food pantries; and support community events along with prayer during harvest and planting seasons.

Outreach for the rural elderly is another example of hope. A congregation in north central Minnesota built a nursing home across from the church. The nursing home is used as a parish center and the rural elderly are incorporated into youth programs, adult education, and caregiving for patients as well as caregivers. This model of church also provides the continuity of one generation to another.

Religious communities that own land are entrusting this land to sustainable agriculture practices and providing models for the community. More and more religious institutions are examining their actions toward land through the prism of their faith tradition and finding that sustainable agriculture, education programs, and helping beginning farmers are in line with their spirituality.[16]

Paired churches of different denominations or "ecumenical shared ministries" are another model of what is happening in rural America. In Busti, New York, American Baptists and United Methodists are successfully sharing a pastor and programs. Presbyterians and Lutherans are sharing numerous congregations in North Dakota. Rural United Church of Christ congregations have been adept at federating with any number of different denominations.

Innovative religious education programs are taking place from seminaries as outreach to rural areas; the North Dakota deacon program in conjunction with Luther Seminary is one good example of innovative training. In addition, identifying new leaders within the rural church—parish administrators, commissioned lay pastors, and others—is a hopeful sign.

In many ways, we are re-visioning what it really means to be church—old patterns are dying. It just might be that rural America is the first place to experience the movement of the Holy Spirit giving birth to new ways of being Christ's church. Through new life there is hope.

The Situation in Rural America

CHAPTER TWO

The History of Rural Church Work

One of the first realizations to which one comes when examining the history of rural churches in the United States and Canada is that until the last decades of the nineteenth century most of American Christianity, and Protestantism in particular, was a rural phenomenon. To a great extent this was due to the history of American settlement. The settlement of what was to become the United States and Canada meant that most churches served rural communities and small towns. Although this pattern had some variety, Christianity in the northern part of the Western Hemisphere had to struggle to meet the demands placed upon it by the European settlement. It needed to develop the mechanisms necessary to ensure that Christianity was transported successfully from settled Europe to "wild" America.[1]

The Colonial Period

While settlement was confined to the eastern side of the Appalachian mountains the settlers were fairly successful at maintaining some similarity of European settlement patterns and organization. This was especially true in New England where legal constraints held sway. There, the process of allotting land for building homes in town and arraying farm acreage around it made possible the establishment of an ordered system for laying out village and rural areas, one modeled on English patterns, that demanded little in the way of adjustments to the distinctive geographic and demographic context.

Similarly, in the middle colonies like Pennsylvania, settlement centered on small towns and was undertaken predominantly by distinctive religious and ethnic groups. This made it much easier for settlers to maintain a close approximation of European settlement patterns and traditional ways of practicing Christianity with little specific attention to the rural context.

The southern colonies presented a different situation, however. With the establishment of African American chattel slavery and the plantation system, the vast distances between residences made the application of the English parish quite difficult, despite the legal establishment of the Church of England in colonies like Virginia. But beyond attempts to recruit priests to serve in Virginia, by the Society for the Propagation of the Gospel in Foreign Parts for example, there was no structural attempt to adjust traditional patterns to meet the distinctive demands of colonial British North America.

The attempts to bring Christianity to French and Spanish North America also faced an immense rural region lacking the basic infrastructure of European settlement or Christian traditions. The responses of the French and Spanish differed markedly from those of the British, however, due to the radically distinctive patterns of settlement in the former's colonies. Since few French or Spanish settlers came to North America, most of the religious work undertaken by them treated America as a foreign land populated by "heathens." Their primary response was to deal with North America as a mission field no different from India or Africa and to work to convert the "natives" and provide chaplains for those forced to serve there.

The Churches and the Frontier

With the establishment of the United States and the opening of western lands for settlement, the various Christian denominations in the United States faced the issue of rural settlement unlimited by legal and social constraints. There was tremendous fear that the new regions to the west would be lost to infidelity or to papacy. Books such as Lyman Beecher's *A Plea for the West* (1835) called upon American Protestantism to meet the challenge and win the West for Christ. The nineteenth century was the heyday of American Protestant expansion, driven largely by the perceived need to bring those who were settling the frontier into the Protestant fold. From this perspective revivalism, voluntary associations, camp meetings, and the circuit rider can be seen as parts of a greater whole—attempts to respond to the realities presented by the increasingly rural nature of American settlement.[2]

Although always a poor relative of foreign missions, the home mission societies were central to the attempts to Christianize America's sparsely settled regions. The nineteenth century saw a profusion of organizations designed to bring the benefits of Christianity and civilization to the entire continent. Although often guilty of conflating American expansionism with Christian truth, these organizations, both denominational and inter-denominational, did much to aid in the settling of what is now the United States. Nearly all of the leading American denominations had established mission societies by the mid-1830s. The Congregationalists had led the way with their several state societies and then merged their efforts with the Presbyterians in the formation of the American Home Missionary Society (A.H.M.S.) in 1826. The Presbyterians, who had formed their national missionary society in 1816, strongly supported the A.H.M.S. while retaining their denominational board. Both the Congregationalists and the Presbyterians were particularly committed to the role of Christianity as a civilizing agent and found their greatest successes in the "Old

Northwest" where most of the early settlers came from New England and the middle states where the two denominations had their strength.

The other leading denominations were not far behind. The Protestant Episcopal Church of America organized its Domestic and Foreign Missionary Society in 1821, following by two years the formation of the Domestic and Foreign Missionary Society of the Methodist Episcopal Church of America. Although the entire denomination was nearly a missionary society of the whole, given its system of itinerancy with its circuit riding ministers, the necessity for an organized response to the immense needs of the frontier was quite obvious.

Of the leading denominations of the time, the Baptists were the last to form a national mission society—the American Baptist Home Missionary Society in 1832. Although conflicts over the nature of salvation and the validity of missions hindered its work somewhat, the society was particularly effective in planting Baptist seeds in rural areas, which would then be tended by local ministers.

While the work of all these societies was disrupted by conflicts over slavery and the resulting Civil War, their successors continued this work up to the present. Many of them, in fact, became the location for the denominations' more formal rural church work in the early 1900s.

Roman Catholics also had to find organized ways to respond to the religious needs of their rural co-religionists. Although most Roman Catholic immigrants to the United States settled in cities, many, especially the Germans, settled in rural areas of the country. They tended to group together in ethnic enclaves, thereby easing the work of organization; nevertheless, there remained the need to ensure that they were served by priests and supplied with the sacraments and religious training. Many bishops and archbishops were attentive to these needs and strove to establish a strong presence among Catholic farmers. Archbishop John Ireland of St. Paul, Minnesota, was only one of the many prelates who took a strong interest in ensuring the maintenance of Roman Catholicism among immigrants. Ireland encouraged immigration to Minnesota and established several agricultural colonies in his archdiocese for immigrants. He was especially concerned that larger numbers of Irish immigrants settle in rural areas, believing that land ownership and farming would keep them out of poverty and moral decline.[3]

Most of the immigrants to the Midwest and Great Plains, however, were Scandinavian Lutherans and German Catholics. They settled these regions by carving out a living from immense spaces and fertile land. In doing so they made their churches the centers of their communal and social lives. For most of these immigrants the church was the link that maintained their ethnic and communal identities. Both the churches and their pastors were rooted in the community and they lived, suffered, and rejoiced with their parishioners. These churches measured the rhythms of life of the farmers and shopkeepers who inhabited the areas. The idea of rural ministry as something distinct and separate was unknown to them. Ministers, priests, and religious attended to their parishioners' needs, just as they would have in any other situation, some well and others badly. Those who did well succeeded because they were attuned to the reality of ministry; they listened to their parishioners and responded to their pain. The churches, however, were not identified only with the ministers or priests. What made these churches successful was the strong identification of the parishioners with them and their closeness to the people.

A similar identification existed in the South as well, especially among Baptists and Methodists. The bi-vocational ministers who predominated in the Southern Baptist Convention experienced the same difficulties and frustrations of their flocks. As a farmer, miner, or laborer during the week and a preacher on Sunday, it was impossible for the minister to be unaware of the lives of their congregants. The rural southern minister, just like the Midwestern pastor, centered his work on meeting spiritual and emotional needs. His message of comfort and support was heeded, not because he explicitly addressed the problems of rural life, but because his knowledge and familiarity of their lives made him a credible voice, regardless of whether he was threatening damnation or offering solace at a funeral.[4]

Despite this real support offered by local ministers and the ongoing concern by denominational and national religious leaders to provide rural areas with the benefits of the gospel and with it the education and civilization which they felt were its natural results, there was little attention to the rural context as such. Certainly there were adjustments to the historical forms and traditional norms that made it easier to bring Christianity to these relatively uninhabited areas. The Methodist circuit riders and the Baptist farmer-preachers proved that flexible models of ministry were more successful in addressing the needs of the frontier. Although the circuit rider was an expediential remedy to a real need, it was not designed primarily with the rural context in mind. In fact, not until the early twentieth century did church leaders explicitly recognize that the rural situation required direct examination and a distinctive set of programs to address what were understood to be the growing problems of America's rural areas.

The Country Life Movement

The first major claim that there was a rural church problem requiring a coordinated response was Charles E. Hayward's *Institutional Work for the Country Church.*[5] Hayward claimed that the decline in rural population was devastating rural communities and especially rural churches, most of which could barely survive this loss. Greater attention was focused on rural America with the 1909 report issued by Theodore Roosevelt's National Commission on Country Life. The report saw the need for greater attention to the "problems" of rural communities. Accepting the view of sociologist Kenyon L.

Butterfield, the report viewed rural churches as having a major role in improving the climate of rural communities.[6]

Although this report saw churches as only part of the overall response to rural needs, it strengthened the hands of the growing number of church leaders who had focused attention on the rural church in the nine years since the publication of Hayward's book. These people believed that the Social Gospel should become a central part of the mission of rural churches. The churches should work to strengthen rural communities by becoming social and communal centers for their communities. Churches should do this not only because it was part of the divine imperative but also because it would be good for their institutional health. Only by finding new ways of bringing people into the churches, they believed, would it be possible for them to survive. The rural population decline was of the utmost concern to many country lifers. They viewed rural areas as terribly over-churched, with populations unable to sustain the existing number of churches in the area even with greater community outreach.

This issue dominated much of the thinking of country lifers; central to their work was the consolidation of denominational churches within a region—usually counties—as well as the creation of union churches, bringing together several churches of varying denominations into one church. They thought that only through such actions could rural churches generate the vitality and resources necessary to act as sources of overall community revitalization. This emphasis may have made some sense given the number of churches in some areas. A survey of rural Jennings County, Indiana, conducted in the early 1920s discovered one church for every 310 people, a marked difference from the one-church-per-thousand most country lifers considered optimal.

However, it did little to endear them to denominational members and leaders. This became particularly significant as denominations began to establish their own departments dedicated to rural work.

The first denomination to establish a department dedicated to working with rural churches was the Presbyterian Church U.S.A. Formed in 1910, the Department of Church and Country Life was a part of the Board of Home Missions and, under its director Warren H. Wilson, modeled the rural life movement's concern with seeing the churches as central to the revitalization of rural communities. It developed demonstration parishes, sponsored training programs for ministers, and funded numerous rural surveys. The department also ran two "Graduate Schools of Religious Sociology," one at the University of Tennessee and another at the University of Wisconsin.

The Presbyterians were followed quickly by other denominations. The Moravian Brethren (1912), the Methodist Episcopal Church (1916), and the Roman Catholic Church (1923). This denominational concern was matched by work on the ecumenical front, including the YMCA, the YWCA, and the Federal Council of Churches. The Federal Council of Churches (the forerunner of the National Council of Churches) created its rural church office in 1912 to act as clearinghouse for rural ministry work and gave George Frederick Wells responsibility for this position. The role of this office increased dramatically in the following year when Gifford Pinchot (the former head of the National Forest Service and one of America's leading early conservationists) offered to fund the Council's work with rural communities. The result was the creation of the Commission on Church and Country Life with Pinchot as chairman, and Charles Otis Gill as Field Secretary. Edmund deS. Brunner, Kenyon L. Butterfield, Warren H. Wilson, and Paul Vogt served as advisors.[7]

The Commission was the most important country life organization in the United States, as was demonstrated at its 1915 conference. Held in Columbus, Ohio, the conference attracted most of the country's leading religious and rural life leaders. Washington Gladden gave the opening invocation, and Gifford Pinchot, Kenyon Butterfield, and Warren H. Wilson were among the featured speakers. The highlight of the conference was a speech by President Woodrow Wilson on "The Rural Church as a Vitalizing Agent."[8]

Nearly all of this work with the rural churches was motivated by the spirit of Progressivism, a desire for social and economic improvement brought about by efficiency, rationality, and planning. Perhaps nothing demonstrated this as much as the movement's use of the survey to identify community needs and problems and its commitment to church consolidation and union churches. These rural surveys were conducted widely throughout the United States and reflected the Progressive belief in the power of knowledge and education in bringing about solutions to social problems. These surveys were not limited only to white Protestant churches. One of the most far-reaching programs of social surveys was directed by W. E. B. Du Bois at Atlanta University. Designed to provide the basis for improving the social and economic situation of African Americans, the project gathered immense amounts of data on African Americans, especially in the rural South. Although the elaborate and detailed recommendations penned by Du Bois and his colleagues in response to this data were ignored, they continued to have a major influence in the organization of programs designed to respond to the needs of rural southern blacks.[9]

The African American Church

Although not particularly visible in the formal rural church movement—given the constraints of legal and cultural segregation—the black churches were significant institutions in the lives of rural blacks, most of whom resided in the southern states. The churches functioned as the most significant cultural institutions, the locations for black self-expression, and the sources of leadership for the black community.

Churches organized many of the services denied or limited to blacks under racist governments in the southern states—including high schools and health care. Additionally, many of the black colleges, such as Tuskegee Institute (now University), combined a strong Christian commitment with a desire to serve the needs of the South's rural blacks.

Despite the constraints imposed by segregation and racism, rural blacks occasionally received the same professional assistance as their white neighbors. A black extension agent, usually working with an historically black college (typically designated an "Agricultural and Mechanical" college), strove to impart information on "scientific" agriculture to those blacks fortunate enough to own or rent farmland. Most blacks, however, were sharecroppers and were forced to raise the dominant cash crop, usually cotton, and therefore were unable to make use of much of the advice, such as practicing crop rotation.

Also central to the mind-set of rural reformers was the commitment to efficiency and rationality in administration and organization. To the reformers it was obvious that if a county could not support all its churches in a viable manner, the only rational thing to do would be to close several churches and merge them into one. This could be done either denominationally (consolidation) or inter-denominationally (union churches). Such actions would make the remaining churches more viable and thereby enable them to meet their obligations to act as centers for the revitalization of their communities. These recommendations aroused opposition among those whose churches were slated for closure and brought the rural commissions into conflict with the denominational leadership who felt that their job was the creation of more Methodist or Presbyterian churches in an area, not consolidating them or, worse, merging them with those of other denominations. In fact, the Methodist Episcopal Church (North) explicitly repudiated the policy of cooperation at its 1924 General Conference meeting.

This decision, and similar ones in other denominations, meant that from the late 1920s through the 1950s, while there remained denominational concern for the rural church as a distinctive entity, there was a decrease in denominational interest in the church as a locus for community improvement. Despite some notable exceptions, rural sociology and rural ministry became increasingly separate. Denominational work with rural churches, however, retained the Progressive emphasis on efficiency, rationality, and standards. The equipment necessary for a modern church and efficient practices were central to much of this work. Ralph A. Felton, who served in the Department of the Rural Church at Drew Theological Seminary, published several pamphlets detailing the requirements of an efficient rural church. In *The Home of the Rural Pastor* he discussed the required furnishings of the pastor's study, the kitchen needs of the pastor's wife, as well as the positive benefits supplied by playground equipment on the parsonage lawn, which itself should be sufficiently large for church socials and picnics. In *The Church Bus* he described the values of a bus ministry, even if it were no more than a converted pickup truck. His *A Study of Voluntary Labor Gifts* reminded the pastor of all the wealth available to him and his church and in *A Hundred Games for Rural Communities* he attempted to address the problem of providing wholesome community entertainment.[10]

While this set of pamphlets did not exhaust his concerns—Felton also wrote of the need for cooperative churches and for church farms—they do illustrate the prevailing tendency to approach rural churches and their communities from the outside. Despite the sincere and true concern that many of these individuals had for rural communities and their residents, much of their work had a missionary tone. They were bringing education, culture, and civilization to the benighted. While this may have been needed, especially in those areas deeply affected by poverty and economic distress, it failed to consider carefully the concerns, values and beliefs of rural church members.

People's commitments to their home church, their distinctive denominational beliefs, and their congregational community were dismissed out of hand as backward and outmoded.

Woman's Work Is Never Done

Although often ignored in the formal histories of rural church work, the role of women in establishing and strengthening congregational life has been immense. Both locally and nationally, women have been among the strongest supporters of home missions. From congregational sewing circles to denominational women's organizations, their concerns and financial support have helped to maintain strong local communities. Historically women provided an immense amount of volunteer labor to their churches which, alongside the fundraising provided by the sale of traditional women's products such as foodstuffs or sewn goods, helped to make many local congregations economically viable.

Women also have been key participants in the numerous reform movements which have been motivated by Christian faith. From anti-slavery to temperance to child-welfare, the role of church women has been key. Today, women are among the first members of rural communities to organize to address local needs. The church needs to support these activities and to work for the equal treatment of women in both church and society.

Such attitudes did not hinder the work of the National Catholic Rural Life Conference. Founded in 1923 the NCRLC shared many of the inward-looking aspects of early twentieth century American Catholicism. Although ecumenical in its willingness to work with others on behalf of improving the quality of rural life, the nature of Roman Catholic church polity prevented the consideration of merging or consolidating Roman Catholic parishes with other churches. This helped save the NCRLC from one of the major difficulties that bedeviled the rural commissions of other denominations. It also kept the organization close to its constituents. Its linkages to the church, which constituted the cement that both held together many rural communities and maintained ethnic and cultural identity, made it less of an alien entity than most Protestant rural life organizations. Even more importantly, the NCRLC could build its work upon the "social encyclicals." These papal documents, most important of which were Leo XIII's *Rerum Novarum* (1891) and Pius XI's *Quadragesimo Anno* (1931), provided a theological basis for church work designed to achieve a more equitable distribution of wealth and, by recognizing the dignity and importance of labor, to guarantee women and men a living wage.[11]

Although there remained specialized departments for work with rural churches staffed by people with deep passion for this work, the post-World War II era saw a marked decrease in the already slight interest in rural communities and greater attention to the suburbs and the cities. This remained true throughout the 1960s and into the 1970s as the nation's attention as well as that of the churches and theologians was focused on America's cities. Much of this shift can be attributed to the very real and growing needs of the cities during that time and the increasing urbanization of the United States. It also reflected a blatant, albeit unstated, perception among many denominational bureaucrats that rural people were hopeless conservatives, who were obstructing the social justice agenda that became increasingly central to most mainline Protestant denominations during those years. The "Farm Crisis" of the 1980s changed this somewhat and altered the approach to rural churches and communities.

The 1980s and Beyond

The problems caused by the "Farm Crisis" of the 1980s occasioned a marked increase in grassroots organizing in rural communities, much of it church-based. Additionally, the growing concern for contextualization of theological and pastoral work influenced many who found themselves assigned to rural churches or placed in situations where they had to address the growing distress of rural communities while simultaneously attending seriously to the distinctive needs and concerns of rural residents.

Another dimension of this revitalization was the growing concern with environmental matters and the pivotal role that rural areas and farmlands had to play in creating a healthy environment. The linkages of such issues as pesticides, non-point of source pollution (fertilizer run-off), sustainable agriculture, and the survival of the family farm brought together varied groups of people who were committed to sustaining and revitalizing rural communities and who viewed rural churches as integral to this revitalization. Unlike the early reformers, however, these people felt that the initiative for and the articulation of the solutions needed to begin with the rural context. Country people had something legitimate and important to say, and while they might occasionally need information from outside, any sustained effort at saving country life had to come from them and had to be something to which they were committed. This merged several traditions in its way of approaching theology. To a great extent this was a logical extension of American democratic thinking, which vested a great deal of wisdom in the people and their decisions. Rooted in the Jeffersonian ideal that also saw the independent farmer as the backbone of the American republic, this approach resonated within the psyche of most rural people and provided them with a sense of importance and significance that most cultural symbols in the United States seemed to deny them.

Additionally, this approach to rural ministry owed much to the organizational work of Saul Alinsky and the Industrial Areas Foundation. Although more directed and normative than Alinsky's model, this work took seriously the needs and aspirations of the people involved and worked with them to address those needs.

Finally, the developing models of rural ministry in the 1980s and 1990s learned from liberation, African American, and feminist theologies that theology has to be contextualized. It has to answer the questions asked by the people who are hearing the gospel at a particular time and in a particular place. This type of theology recognizes that when the child asks for bread one does not give a stone. As a result theological and religious activity is a constant interchange between the questions and needs of a particular people in a particular place and the answers of the Gospel. When this occurs the Christian mystery of the incarnation becomes possible in people's lives.

A symbol of this realization is the growing number of seminary-based programs that assist seminarians in preparing for the realities of rural parishes and helping them appreciate the strengths of their parishioners. Such work will go far toward strengthening these churches and their communities as well as providing a more satisfying pastoral experience for all.

Greater attention to the particular realities of the rural context is only part of the issue, however. Since many rural and small town churches have small memberships and denominations can do little to support these congregations or their ministers, it is increasingly difficult for these churches to obtain and maintain ministers. Additionally, many of those minsters who do serve those churches tend to view their tenure as "time-serving" while they await a larger or more prestigious post. This negative view of rural churches is exacerbated by the fact that most seminarians who had a strong denominational/congregational commitment before entering seminary tend to come from suburban, big steeple churches and are as unfamiliar with the rural context as they are with the inner city. Many seem to feel that God has called them to a suburban church.

While seminary programs designed to identify individuals concerned with rural ministry and to assist seminarians in finding ways to adjust to the rural context are helpful, they cannot address all the needs of rural churches especially in the near-term. Many congregations, local judicatories, and even denominations are looking at creative means of responding to those needs. One of the most promising is the growing attention paid to lay and bi-vocational ministry. Not only do these programs provide a greater opportunity for churches that otherwise would have empty altars to be served by a minister, they also call forth from congregations greater levels of accountability and involvement. By moving the central responsibility for the life of the church away from the ordained minister, these models of ministry locate ministry in the whole body of the faithful. Although the seeming novelty of this can result in many difficulties and problems, individual congregations that take on these new responsibilities often experience new life.

The turn to lay ministers presents numerous organizational difficulties for many denominations. Not only does it require a major re-thinking of the discipline and order of the church, but also careful attention to issues of church "citizenship," if lay ministers and the congregations they serve are not going to be relegated to the back of the church bus. Congregations in those denominations that limit the administering of the sacraments or ordinances to ordained ministers must ensure that these elements of religious life can be made available to churches with lay pastors. While these issues and the responses to them may seem somewhat novel, they harken back to earlier periods in the church's life. From the Middle Ages to the seventeenth century much of Europe was served by traveling priests and many people received the sacraments only once or twice a year. Additionally, in the United States, Methodists historically received the sacraments only on those occasions when the ordained circuit rider was in town. During the rest of the time the local congregations were sustained by the lay teacher.

Another response to this reality is the return to the idea of cooperative parishes. Rather than an enforced closure or merger of churches, these new cooperative ministries emerge from the local recognition that only by combining resources and energies can the needs of the local community be met. The result is not always a merger of two churches, but often a process of partnership among churches which maintain separate identities, to address particular realities or gaps in services. To function well, however, these ministries require an informed laity willing and able to take an active role in their own Christian lives.

As most denominations begin to face economic and institutional retrenchment, local congregations, mid-level judicatories, and para-church organizations increasingly must produce creative responses to contemporary needs. While denominational bureaucracies will continue to have a role to play in the future of rural ministry, their present reality makes it unlikely that they can create the coordinated and organized response that emerged in the early 1900s in the Country Life Movement. While much may be lost because of this inability, positively it means that the religious responses to the needs and vitality of rural life will come from those people and from those who attend carefully to their lives and whose familiarity with the rural scene gives them the ability to craft a response. Indeed the future seems to rest with those congregations that strive to discern and realize God's providence and power within the context of their communities.

CHAPTER THREE

Seeing Rural America in Context

"America the Beautiful" is a hymn of tribute to our North American continent and to its Creator. For some this stirring music calls forth strong images of natural and cultivated beauty; for others it evokes memories of pride and commitment associated with the dark days of World War II. Traveling across this land we have had the image of beauty confirmed again and again. America is indeed the beautiful. America the Beautiful.

The natural *beauty of place* is multifaceted. Colors, smells, sounds, shadows, contrasts, textures, seasons, and surprises fill the land, lakes, and seascapes. Each area has its own God-given beauty: the glistening white coldness of the Arctic north, birds flitting across a sea marsh, wild flowers in the spring, autumn leaves, the roar of a waterfall, the frolicking of newborn creatures, the sounds of nightfall around an isolated farmstead, the colors of a western sunset, a rainbow, the sweet smell after a spring shower, a herd of cattle across a field of winter wheat, the noise of children at play in a village schoolyard.

Often one finds a *beauty in the built places*, as well. New England villages, well-ordered mill towns, neat farmsteads, Amish barns, the parade of elevator towns at six mile intervals across the Cornbelt, the pueblos of the Southwest, fishing villages on the northern coasts, majestic plantation houses, and country churches are among the built places in which we find beauty. How does your list go?

The people of the land are also *beautiful of body, culture, and spirit*. Because of the historic settlement pattern of North America, various racial and ethnic groups are clustered in its several regions. While there is the beauty of youthful expectation in each group, there is also a beauty of face and hands about those whose life has been well-lived. There is a beauty in the rituals of everyday greeting, sharing, and leave-taking in the cafes, post offices, courthouses, stores, and churches of rural America. There is a beauty in the responses to crisis and tragedy as neighbors and kin rush to care for one another. The annual celebrations and festivals of the people in the places are beautiful: powwows, tractor pulls, rodeos, fairs, Octoberfests, Christmas pageants, and Fourth of July celebrations. Many of these places still run on a rhythm that offers an appealing sense of continuity to life.[1]

Not a few times we have been brought up short by the *beauty of spirit* among the people of rural America—

- Deep, abiding faith in the sovereignty and providence of God, even in the face of Job-like suffering.
- Lives changed radically by an encounter with God.
- Caring concern for those who hurt and suffer all around the world.
- Worship that addresses the realities of everyday life among the members of the congregation.
- Congregational life that is multi-ethnic; i.e., "red and yellow, black and white" as many of us sang, but did not experience, in our early days of religious training.

In short, many town and country congregations exhibit the faith, hope, and love that the Apostle Paul wrote to the Corinthian church about (1 Cor. 13). The qualities of unity, purity, mutual submission and focused activity that he told the church at Ephesus were to characterize the family of God are found there (Eph. 1–4). In many town and country churches we have found the most faithful approximation of these qualities of New Testament church life.

America the Ugly

Other songs speak of life in rural America, also. They tell the story of infidelity, violence, and rape of persons and places. African American spirituals were often veiled songs of protest. So are the labor songs from the Appalachian coal camps. They identify social or institutional sin.

Slavery, Indian wars, and blood feuds were integral elements of life in rural America in an earlier age. So was the exploitation of coal miners, millhands, and yeoman farmers by corporate America. Today, many find similar patterns in petro-chemical-based agriculture, strip mining, vertically integrated agriculture, toxic waste dumping, pollution of air, land, and water, clear-cut timbering, and many other uses and abuses of rural places and peoples by American and world corporations. Social sin abounds, indeed.

Personal and interpersonal sin also abounds in rural America. Some rural folk violate the laws of God with reckless abandon. "Good" folk who have blind spots in their values and/or find themselves explaining away the evil they do are there in large numbers. Some abuse themselves, their families, and/or the environment. Some fail to worship God. Others worship in the hope that they can get God to do what they want for their projects.

Yes, there is much to do as a minister in rural America. Many persons have rejected and/or neglected to come to faith in Jesus Christ and accept the grace he offers. Many are not obedient to his teachings. Others are not active in the life of their church. Further, social structures, traditions, and practices fall far short of biblical norms. In many instances, these social sins will be present within the life of the church(es) that you serve. These need to be addressed.[2]

Yes, America is also ugly. It has been "uglified" by the way the natural environment has been exploited. It has been uglified by the sins we commit in our relationships with one another. It has been uglified by the policies of governments and corporations, which have seen persons and places as expendable. It has been uglified by an unwillingness to count "personal," environmental, and social costs as part of the equation for doing business in God's world. It has been uglified by a bad theology that does not take seriously the plain teachings of Scripture that God expects justice and mercy, particularly for the poor, the widows and orphans, and the aliens in the land (Pss. 1; 24; 103; 146).

Churches, local and national, are not without sin here. Often the local church has become too identified with the local culture and its sins, and has lost its prophetic voice. It blesses a culture more than challenges it. Often the national denominations have seen many of their town and country churches as provincial and quaint, too small, too weak, or too poor.

The role of pastors in town and country places, then, must include both affirmation of the beauty and recognition of the ugliness of American rurality. As a prophet, the pastor denounces the ugliness of sin—personal, interpersonal, and corporate. This includes both the sins of the people and of the place, and the sins of others directed toward his/her people and place. The prophetic pastor announces the perfect will of God for people and for place. As a priest, she/he deals with the hurts and the guilt and anger resulting from all this sin. She hears confession; he offers good counsel; she mediates forgiveness and grace; he offers healing and hope. As a representative of the Sovereign, the rural pastor works to reformulate policies, structures, and practices, bringing them in line with the absolutes of God, as much as is possible in a free and pluralistic society. As an evangelist, he declares the gospel of grace. It is a difficult role. It is an exciting role. It is an emerging role.

In the sections that follow, we treat America and the world as being in one of those "hinge-times" of change. The paradigm will be different in the next century. If God directs your life toward long-term commitment to town and country ministry, you will be one of the re-visioners of rural ministry. You will take what is constant in the role of pastor or lay leader and apply it to a new context.

The Stock of Rural U.S. Churches

The initial step in the re-visioning process is for us to have a clear understanding of the "stock" of rural churches currently present in non-metropolitan America. As many as 200,000 congregations serve the rural USA. These vary in size from less than ten to several thousand members or participants. In 1990, the Church Membership Survey (CMS) researchers identified 116,872 congregations in the non-metropolitan counties. This report, published as *Churches and Church Membership in the United States, 1990*, presents data collected from most of the church bodies in the nation.[3]

We believe that the total number of "rural" churches, however, is closer to 200,000 than to the 116,872 reported for at least three reasons. First, several denominations with significant rural memberships did not participate actively in the study. For example, most African-American congregations are absent from the count. Second, by using county-based data, thousands of congregations were swept up in the metro church count that by culture, and/or by location actually continue to be rural churches although they are located within a county designated as metropolitan. The third concern has already been suggested but must be stated clearly. "Rural" refers both to place and to culture. Often they overlap, but not always. So, to identify churches as metro, or as non-metro, here only notes location. It may miss the actual culture and self-identity of the church. Even with these reservations, the CMS data provides us with the best quantitative picture of the distribution and membership of rural churches in the U.S. available to us, so we will use it.

TABLE 3.1

The CMS totals for 1980 and 1990 by churches and adherents for most of the major U.S. denominations. These are the non-metropolitan county figures:

Denomination name	Congregations		Adherents	
	1980	*1990*	*1980*	*1990*
American Baptists/USA	2,178	2,022	487,004	451,784
AME Zion	770	850	277,451	301,456
Assemblies of God	4,180	4,583	472,693	540,634
Baptist General Conference		250		35,800
Baptist Missionary Association		937		171,711
C & M Alliance		529		65,721
Christian Church/Church of Christ	2,796	2,577	485,904	475,225
Christian Reformed		227		61,721
Church of God—Anderson		1,016		80,118
Church of God—Cleveland	2,272	2,230	181,138	244,369
Church of the Brethren		576		82,104
Church of the Nazarene	2,070	2,101	286,339	280,050
Churches of Christ	6,830	6,790	627,938	601,580
Disciples of Christ	2,099	1,904	449,990	376,387
Episcopal Church	2,269	2,324	401,494	347,896
Evangelical Free		398		45,425
Evangelical Lutheran	4,500	4,436	1,691,038	1,629,505
Free Will Baptist		1,397		159,624
Friends		510		36,343

Denomination name	Congregations		Adherents	
	1980	*1990*	*1980*	*1990*
Foursquare Gospel		437		45,153
Latter Day Saints	2,523	2,986	794,753	924,438
Lutheran—Missouri Synod	2,404	2,512	804,750	807,773
Lutheran—Wisconsin Synod		575		184,756
Mennonite Church		525		57,866
Old Order Amish		576		84,095
Pentecostal Holiness		825		75,208
Presbyterian Church in America		360		39,188
Presbyterian/USA	5,091	4,424	896,142	775,768
Reformed Church in America		258		96,169
Roman Catholic	8,154	8,181	5,985,243	6,141,767
Salvation Army		379		32,283
Seventh Day Adventist		1,709		178,794
Southern Baptist	19,453	20,227	6,397,621	7,153,937
Unitarian-Universalist		224		18,240
United Church of Christ	2,287	2,198	486,880	466,915
United Methodist	20,816	19,783	4,162,340	3,813,979
Wesleyan Church		794		103,880

Nearly three-fourths of the counties of the U.S. are non-metro. About one person in five dwells in these counties, or in 1990 almost 51 million. This was a gain of about 1.3 million in the decade of the 1980s. It is estimated that the non-metro population grew another 1.3 million in the first three years of the 1990s.

The 116,872 congregations identified by the CMS researchers count 31.5 million members/adherents, or about 60 percent of the non-metro county population. Given the point made earlier that thousands of rural congregations are not captured in the CMS report, the numbers of "adherents" may pass the 40 million mark and the percentage rise up to 80 percent or even more. While the numbers are high, it is not the case that the evangelism and outreach work of the churches in rural America is virtually complete. Not at all. Likewise, although the ratio of churches to population runs 1:450 using the CMS data, and is probably more like 1:350, this does not mean, necessarily, that no more are churches needed in non-metro places. Really, one can only conclude that the rural churches have been effective in gaining adherents by whatever means their tradition affirms, and that while some rural areas may be "over-churched," this does not allow for the conclusion that the rural U.S., as such, is over-churched.

Roman Catholics comprise the only major U.S. Christian ecclesiastical body that is more metropolitan in membership composition than is the nation. Yet, while only 12.7 percent of its adherents are non-metro, because of its huge total size, it ranks second behind Southern Baptists in the actual number of rural adherents. It seems that because Roman Catholics are such a visible force in metropolitan America, many of us lose sight of the fact that they are such an important player in rural areas as well.

Among the many valuable insights to be drawn from CMS maps is that in most counties one denomination has emerged as the dominant one. Settlement patterns by race and ethnicity as well as the charisma of certain persons in the era of rapid rural church planting (essentially the nineteenth century) explain much of this. We note the Roman Catholic dominance around the coastal edges of the nation and in a strip up the eastern bank of the Rockies, and Lutheran dominance in many corn and wheat region counties. The United Methodists, mixed with some Disciples presence, are numerous across the midlands. Mormons continue to dominate their traditional Inland Empire. And there is a heavy concentration of Baptists across the South and Southwest stretching up into Missouri and southern Illinois in the Midwest. [4]

With revived population growth in many more non-metro counties continuing in the 1990s, it seems very likely that many denominations could observe significant numbers of their congregations growing. We believe that the swelling tide of urban to rural migration, the coming of the Information Age, and the revitalizing of rural communities and churches offer a promising future for rural missions and church work in many regions of the nation.

Toffler's Typology

Now, against this backdrop, we present a three-fold typology developed by Alvin Toffler in *The Third Wave* to explain the historic and the apparent future trends of life in North America. He writes about three waves of sociocultural and community development: agricultural, industrial, and informational. The first was the wave of settlement of the continent as homesteads were claimed and villages formed. The nineteenth century was the focal period for this wave. The second was the movement of people to the industrializing cities. The twentieth century experienced most of the power of this era. The third wave is the current decoupling and recoupling of job and residency being made possible by the emergence of advanced information technology. Significant numbers are electing to move from the cities to town and country America. Much of the twenty-first century will experience the force of this engine of change (feet, freeways, and fiber optics are the primary modes of movement in each wave). Toffler's typology provides a useful tool for organizing and understanding the context for contemporary rural ministry.[5]

Typologies are useful tools but hurtful masters. They are helpful in organizing great masses of material, and in identifying trends of history. But they can oversimplify and distort. And they can be used to suggest that certain trends are inevitable, becoming self-fulfilling prophecies.

In America, churches (denominations) can be viewed as social institutions with divine mandates. They came into existence in a particular place and time. They seek to be faithful to a tradition (and/or a new vision, or a recapturing of the old vision) and to be effective within their context. Contexts change across time. New and different people may come to live in the region. Technological changes may alter how the people in a context earn their living and how the rhythm of everyday life runs. The church adapts. Radical societal paradigm shifts come along occasionally. These major shifts are what Toffler identifies with his three waves. Responding to these shifts is particularly tricky. It is informative to consider how many of the denominations listed in Table 3.1 arose in the hinge-times of paradigm shifts, some in reaction to change, some as proponents of change. That became evident in Chapter Two. These great shifts reorder values and worldviews. Conflicts arise. Should we reject, adapt, accept, or redirect? The growth of new charismatic and some independent churches in our time reflects, in part, the dynamics of the hinge-time we are now experiencing.

Against All Odds

In *Against All Odds* (Westview, 1994), John Allen and Don Dillman attempt to analyze the impact of the coming of the Information Age on a small farm/ranch service town in the Northwest. What they found was an interesting blending of the technology of the third wave with the customs and practices of the first and second. They give some attention to all of the social institutions, including the churches.

Local churches also find themselves grappling with changes in their context. Most of the changes are small. They can be organized for analysis and understanding around the POET rubric—people, organizations, environment, and technology. But occasionally a huge wave of change crashes over us. Many of the thousands of rural churches in the US came into existence because of what Toffler identifies as the first wave. What many of these churches do, programmatically, is grounded in the impact of Toffler's second wave. However, the rural church today is in a hinge point of time again. On the one hand, it must respond to the challenges presented by the end products of the second wave, while gearing up to respond to the third wave. Those who work with rural churches in the next few decades will need to be especially creative and innovative persons. Three or four areas of special challenge can be identified at this time.

- Rural America will need to be re-churched, in terms of focus, activities, location, and patterns of pastoral leadership. Electronic media will make it possible for the very best Christian resources to be provided in very remote places. Very urbane persons will be able to elect to live in very rural locations and will want appropriate congregational life. And there will be increasing numbers of persons who will need to be evangelized and assisted in committing their lives to Jesus as Lord and Savior.

- Rural America will need to reformulate its community life. While we cannot return to the forms of community that served the Agrarian Age, we still need community. On the one hand, the rural churches can model community. On the other, they can provide vision and leadership for the new forms.

- Rural America will need to model environmentally sustainable and renewable life. Hopefully, as information replaces material production on center stage of the economy, the pressure on the material world may lessen.

The biblical concept of stewardship will come to the prominence it deserves in guiding everyday life.

How to Define a Rural Church

The following categories may be helpful in identifying the issues that are animating your church, and some of the recent limits and future opportunities that your church enjoys.

By location: Ribbonville, Agraville, Mighthavebeenville (including open country), Fairview, in a city (These terms are defined in Chapter Four.)

By model vocations for membership: Farmers and ranchers, bivocational (farmers and ranchers with city employment), other extraction workers (miners, fishermen, oil patch workers, loggers), merchants and professionals who serve an extraction-based community and its people, retirees from the extraction industries, and milltown and other small town factory workers, etc.

By SES (Socio-economic status): Poor folk, marginally-making-it folk, substantial folk, community-elite folk, in-but-not-of folk (commuters/retirees), and mixed

By racial/ethnic origins: English, German, Scandinavian, Eastern European, Southern European, Native American, Hispanic, other Latin, Asian, African-American, mixed, and other

By denominational families: Roman Catholic, Lutheran, Orthodox Catholic, Mainline, Baptists, old Pentecostal/Holiness, new Charismatic, and cults

By size of the church (active adults): Very small (less than 50), small (50–110), mid-sized (111–225), and larger (226 and over)

By role in the community: Dominant, distinctive, denominational

By field: Township, county, vocation or interest, family

By focus of ministry: Care of members, revivals, conversionism, social services, social issues, community leadership

---

The First Wave and Rural Church Network

The first wave was the age of Agrarianism. Its guiding paradigm was the dream of President Thomas Jefferson that the nation would be comprised of yeoman farmers and shop-keepers. The new western lands were surveyed out in town-ships, usually six mile by six mile squares. Farm families would settle on tracts within the township. The Agrarian dream called for the creation of a village near the center of the township.[6] Here twenty five to thirty five families of persons providing services for the farm families would live. In this fashion, community centers would be formed about every six miles in which the residents could take care of most of their needs and offer for sale the surplus production of their farms. The plan-tation system in much of the South was somewhat different, although the larger ones took on elements of this village configuration of services.

The story of domestic or home missions during the Agrar-ian Age of the first wave was the story of planting churches in the township villages and hamlets because it was in the town and country places that most Americans lived well into the current century. The often-cited fact that only in 1920 did more citizens of the United States live in urban rather than rural areas is somewhat misleading in that urban refers to places of 2,500 and above. In fact, many of the smaller urban places continued to be essentially rural in orientation and culture. So it could be argued that the balance shifted only after World War II from rural to metropolitan residency.[7] (Whether or not the national culture has become truly "urbanized," more urbanized, or interestingly mixed with the rural, is still subject to debate.)

As settlement marched across the continent, so did mission-aries and evangelists. Informed by the parish concept of Europe, the dominant model was to have a church or churches serving each township. For the denominational bodies with deep roots on the European continent, this meant settling a well-trained missionary/pastor in the emerging towns. Usually, they focused on rounding up those who had adhered to their church denomination across the Atlantic or in the colonies to form a local congregation. The Methodists, Baptists, some Presbyterians, and the new denominations that appeared on the frontier (Disciples, Church of God, Cumberland Presbyterian) relied more on missionary/evangelists who typically gathered congregations from the unchurched on the frontier, then raised up within the congregation an indigenous pastor whom they mentored. It was common for these itinerant evangelists to conduct a revival meeting in a community and form the converts into a congregation. Many thousands of country crossroads Methodist, Baptist, and Disciple congregations began in just this way as the old Northwest Territory and the Louisiana Purchase were being settled.

Today, many Caucasian Protestant town and country churches, particularly those in open country and village settings, are the descendants of those nineteenth-century first wave congregations. They still see their parish or "church field" as the township or three miles in each direction. Often, because of declining farm and village population, the little church is left with only a handful of current and potential members. Many of these churches have died or been consolidated. Many others have become a "family" chapel, serving mostly a kinship clan. Many current seminarians will have as her or his first charge just such a church. The church is an institutional expression of a former community. With the collapse of that community does the church, or should the church, have a future? Does consolidation work? Does federation work? Is there another paradigm that might be applied to this reality?

Yet Caucasians were not the only residents of the American frontier. Some were Native Americans. Others were enslaved African-Americans. Baptists, and to a lesser extent Methodists, in the South experienced great success in evangelizing these peoples. High on any list of explanations for this is the fact that these denominations encouraged the raising up of indigenous leadership. Prior to the Civil War most Baptist and Methodist congregations in the slave states had African-American members. Often they were the numerical majority. With freedom there was an explosion of new racially homogeneous congregations. Motives were certainly mixed. In several instances the existing church building was deeded to the African-American congregation and the whites formed a second church.

Among the five major tribes of the South, several Native American chiefs and clan leaders became Baptist or Methodist preachers. For the southern Indians, removal to the West after 1838, and for the slaves, Emancipation in 1863, seemed to spur the formation of local congregations led by the indigenous leaders with some limited fraternal connection with the missionary/evangelists from the Baptist and Methodist Home Mission Boards.

Events in Europe in the late 1840s, political unrest, war, and famine stimulated massive migration to America. Many of these persons were Roman Catholic or Lutheran. Several Catholic mission societies and orders had long been engaged in evangelizing the Native Americans of the North and the West. With some structure in place, particularly in the key western cities of New Orleans, Saint Louis, and Chicago, the Catholics moved quickly to form congregations of Germans and the Irish on the frontier. The Lutheran story is one having to deal with old ethnic rivalries that were carried to the new land. At the end of the nineteenth century, there were more than a dozen different Lutheran Synods or denominational groups active on the frontier, often in competition with one another. Ethnic tensions were present, but less visible, among the Catholics.

In the last quarter of the nineteenth century, further waves of Catholics, Lutherans, and Anabaptists moved into the Heartland region of America. Pushed by persecution and drawn by cheap land, they came. Often they settled in rather homogeneous township-based communities. For example, as one travels out across that region, one finds towns still dominated by German Catholics, Swedish, Danish, or Norwegian Lutherans,

Dutch Reformed, German/Russian Mennonites, and the like. Even after more than a century, significant elements of the old culture are strong, though melded with elements of the American culture.[8]

In the coal-producing areas of Appalachia this monocultural village planting was also a common feature of the late nineteenth century. Italian-, Russian-, Welsh-, and Polish-dominated villages were formed by the developers of the mines. An appropriate church was formed and partially supported by the mining company. Often the town had a second church, one for the Anglo management, merchants, and other professionals.

In summary, the stock of rural churches, the shape of denominational distribution and strength in rural America, and the concept that the church is to evangelize, nurture, and minister within the bounds of its township (three miles in each direction from its doors) are deeply rooted in the first wave settlement of the continent. Several new American denominations and religious bodies emerged on the frontier in part as a response to this great mission task. And the religious life of America became much richer and more complex as a result of immigration from Europe to the frontier. The southwestern United States is not treated in this summary because its core settlement was in place before the nineteenth century. There, Roman Catholic missionaries converted the native people and established a regional hegemony that has only begun to be diluted by the influx of new people into the rural Southwest.[9]

The Rural Church in the Second Wave Era

Toffler's second wave denotes the growth of cities from the mid-nineteenth century on to the present. It focuses on the expansion of cities at the expense of the countryside in land, people, influence, and power. The way of the factory became the organizing principle of everyday life. When the cities began to grow because of industrialization, a common model was to build a factory and cluster around it housing for the workers and for management. The concept was an adaptation of the English mill village. Many early industrial cities were essentially collections of mill villages; e.g. Birmingham, Alabama. Generally, for the first two generations of this era, the village church model simply was moved to the city. The urban mill villages had a chapel or two for the workers. It duplicated many of the practices of the rural village church. The primary difference was that the seasons and rhythms of the industry replaced the seasons of the soil at the center of the life of the congregation. This sameness was appropriate because the new urbanites were mostly ex-ruralites.

Further, as the city grew the Old First Church in the downtown area became the status church for its denomination. It drew the more affluent and upwardly mobile adherents from across the city.[10] In time church types differentiated so that contemporary observers could categorize them as being essentially one or the other: evangelistic, social concern, pillar, social ministry, and sanctuary in focus.[11] Further, many denominations adapted the language and the methods of the factory to local church life. Distinctively urban, task-oriented ways of doing church developed alongside the relational ways and rhythms of rural church life. The developing urban dominance of society played itself out in at least three ways in rural church and community life.

First, as these cities grew, they moved out into surrounding townships. There a country or village church would find itself becoming a suburban one. The development of the interstate system since World War II, white flight, the suburbanization of industry and the multi-nucleation of the megalopolises have all accelerated this process in recent time. Many of these ex-rural congregations have struggled to resolve conflict between first wave and second wave thinking. To wit: how does one blend and bond relational persons (rural) with task-oriented persons (metropolitan)?

Second, the primary communal paradigm of the second wave was termed "mass society." It means that the local control of the first wave rural community has been lost. Its life is dominated by regional, national, or even global institutions. Another contention of Vidich and Bensman in *Small Town in Mass Society* (1958) is that rural/urban differences were being eroded. Modernity would make the city cousin and the country cousin alike. For national denominations this played out in the curtailment of "rural church programs." In time it became fashionable to distinguish, rather, between large and small churches. Size was seen as more significant than place in understanding the culture of a congregation.[12]

Third, in reflecting upon their first rural pastorates in the 1950s and 1960s some pastors and denominational workers realize now that they went out from the seminary about as much a missionary of modernity as they were a pastor and preacher of the gospel. In their kit were the basic tools from the denomination's publishing house. *Standardization* was the watchword. It was believed that one should be able to attend churches of a given denomination on successive Sundays in Charleston, Chicago, Casper, and Capistrano and find people studying the Bible from the same quarterly, singing hymns from the same book, and listening to sermons that sounded very much the same.

At its worst, this second wave era of industrialization resulted in a kind of "urban imperialism" that has alienated many rural Christians from their denominations. At its best, it helped the churches to grow and prosper from the end of World War II to the mid 1960s by adapting second wave life ways to church life. The new convert could quickly assimilate, for the church "world" was structured after the pattern of her/his work world.

It has been interesting to note that in the hinge-time at the end of the nineteenth century, as society was moving from the first to the second wave, the Protestant denominations that had been most effective in terms of growth during the first wave were deeply troubled by strife and defection. It was then among the Methodists, Baptists, and Disciples that waves of Fundamentalist, Holiness, Pentecostal, and Independent groups emerged. In general, they opposed education, modernity, centralization, urbanity, rationalization, and routinization. In short, they resisted movement into the era of the second wave. Leadership and strong support for this reaction came from the rural churches, including those located in the cities. (One might argue that the seeming antipathy of current denominational leaders toward rural church may be grounded in this perceived adversarial relationship.) If this assessment is correct, can much of the ferment in the denominations of the U.S. today be attributed to the fact that we are now in the hinge-time of moving to the era of the third wave?

The fact is that the "pot never melted." So, today we speak of a "garden salad" in which people's differences are affirmed. Cultural diversity has replaced massification as the societal norm. This is reflected in the third wave that is washing upon this day, giving us what Toffler has called "future shock." It is shocking to first wave congregations and denominations. It is shocking to second wave congregations and denominations as well. It seems to follow that a major task for the coming generation of church leaders will be to discover the appropriate forms of congregational and denominational life for vitality in the third wave. Yet, while this is being done, all of those first and second wave churches out there will need leadership.

If the "place" or parish was the primary (along with denominational or theological stance and ethnic identity) organizing principle of congregational formation in the era of the first wave, "programs" tended to be the principle in the second. People began to seek out a church that "met their needs" even when this meant driving out of their community and/or switching denominations. If they did not "feel" they were getting something they wanted from church involvement, they either dropped out or went elsewhere. The relative newness of city communities and their limited bondedness has made this more common in urban places, but it is common in rural communities today as well.

Conclusion

For many contemporary pastors and seminarians, their career path may lead through churches of one wave to another. Others will be drawn toward congregations of a particular wave. And still others may find themselves acting as an "agent of change" moving a church from one wave to another. Examples of all three wave churches can be found in rural settings. Thousands of small open country and village congregations are still primarily first wave churches. Often these churches are referred to as "family chapels." Second wave churches are those town and country churches that faithfully perform all of the program ideas suggested by their denomination. Often they are larger and better resourced than the first wave family chapel. In some instances, they have grown very large and are a town and country expression of the urban megachurch. An example of the rural third wave church might be one that targets the urban retirees at a lake, "ex-urban cowboys," "cottage industries" workers, or home schoolers across a country in thirty-mile circles. Such churches attempt to reach a more specific, more narrowly defined set of people from a much larger territory than the parish church did.

In this chapter we have attempted to give an estimate of the stock of churches that serve rural America. We noted that while it is large and diverse, demographic developments indicate much challenging work needs to be done. We also noted how most areas of the nation are dominated by a particular denominational family and suggested how this came to be. Finally, we employed the three waves typology developed by futurist Alvin Toffler to provide a means for grasping the culture one finds in many rural churches and to underscore the opportunities and challenges in rural ministry. Again, let us stress that we see the next decade or two as a time when creative, innovative persons will need to create new forms of church life in rural America.

Alex Sim's book, *Land and Community,* offers a healthy sense of the diversity of rural places and also of the creative possibilities for church life.[13] His way of describing these places and churches offers a tool that enables ministers and laypeople in this hinge-time at the end of the second wave to find focus and direction for their efforts at providing leadership in town and country churches and communities. Our next chapter will use his typology and apply it to the rural United States in an effort to locate issues that are emerging there and to describe Toffler's third wave a bit more.

CHAPTER FOUR

Understanding Your Congregation and Community

Canadian sociologist and churchman R. Alex Sim has developed a typology for identifying the shape and condition of town and country community life at the end of the twentieth century—Ribbonvilles, Agravilles, Mighthavebeenvilles, and Fairviews.[1] His description will assist clergy and lay leaders to understand the setting in which their congregations are located as well as the issues that are emerging there.

Ribbonville

Sim labels those small towns in the counties that surround a city (collar counties), "Ribbonvilles." Most were once township, six-mile square, trade centers for yeoman farmers. But as New York City, Atlanta, Houston, Chicago, Los Angeles, and the like have sprawled out across the countryside they have gobbled up village after village. Usually, in a decade or two these Ribbonvilles are transformed from free-standing villages into an integral part of the city. For example, as the map below indicates, going east from downtown Atlanta one finds the former villages of Decatur, Clarkston, Stone Mountain, and Snellville incorporated into metropolitan Atlanta. On farther lie the towns of Loganville, Between, and Monroe. The first two are Ribbonvilles. Suburban homes on small acreages are appearing. Small subdivisions are being platted and homes put up. Schools are crowded. New ones are being built. Strip malls spring up. Farmers are selling out and moving their operations. A proposed second perimeter highway will bisect Loganville early next century. An "edge city" will appear there.[2] Atlanta will become not sixty but one hundred miles in diameter. Monroe will become a Ribbonville with residents commuting both toward Atlanta and toward Athens.

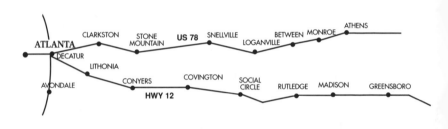

Literally hundreds of congregations that are now rural and village, first and second wave, will be confronted by a significantly altered context. As a result, almost in the shadow of gerry-built Turner's Chapel founded in 1832 with its wraparound cemetery—where seven generations of Turners lie in the ground and three generations now worship—quarter-and half-million-dollar homes are springing up. Will the new community residents and the Turners be able to blend in worship in this church? Will this first wave church become a second wave congregation? Or will the churches in the village of Loganville, which embrace elements of first and second wave thinking, become second wave churches, even emerging megachurches as programs take over as the integrating factor in the congregations? Or will the churches continue to hold to the ties and bonds of place and multi-generational relationship, rejecting the industrial age, programmatic approach that seems to appeal most to the newcomers to their community?

The church mix in Ribbonvilles will also be impacted by the relocation of older city congregations to their area, but with little attachment to the place. Denominational agencies will likely select Loganville for placement of a "new franchise." Then, too, one or more of the old village churches may decide that the best response to their new neighbors may be to bless the forming of a new congregation which targets these new folk. So, in places such as Loganville there will be four or five varieties of the congregations related to the denominations that have been there for a long time, and some new denominational congregations, and some non-denominational ones as well. The hegemony of the dominant denomination may well be broken and a new ecclesiological ecology developed.

All across North America, out along the corridors from the cities, are Ribbonvilles, those places in transition from rural to urban. Rapid change characterizes these places. One day Turner's Chapel may be an urban church, or more probably, it may continue to be a rural church in an urban setting. One day the village or the town church in Ribbonville may take on a culture very different from its current one. The major concern of most of these churches will be how to respond to the heightened diversity of their places. Is there only one possible response, or are several responses appropriate? In an earlier time most would have declared that the church should change. Today some are declaring that each church must seek God's will for itself, while allowing and encouraging diverse congregations. For example, maybe it is really all right for Turner's Chapel to continue to be what it has long been, as long as it does not keep more urban-oriented congregations from moving in or starting up and serving their new neighbors. And it would also be all right for Pilgrim's Rest to conclude that it should change and become more inclusive of its new neighbors as it is for Old First to sponsor Immanuel as a new congregation for new people.

Ribbonville is a part of town and country America, but increasingly less so. It is an exciting and challenging place in which to do ministry.

Agraville

Sim's second type of contemporary rural community is what he terms Agraville. He has in mind those farm service towns in which Wal-Mart and/or K-Mart have set up shop. The economic base of an Agraville is most likely in agriculture, but it may also include extractive activities such as mining or forestry and associated industries. Typically, they have from 2,500 to 50,000 residents and as many as 100,000 in their 30-mile diameter trade area. But this is a very broad range. Those who get much beyond 15,000 or 20,000 residents are now termed micropolitan because they are more like city than like town.[3] The Agravilles are often out on the highway corridors from the cities, beyond the Ribbonvilles. Although impacted by "mass society" they seem to have a distinct existence of their own. They often think that they are still in control. Often the Agravilles seem confident and proud because they have come to dominate their county and perhaps even portions of their neighboring counties. People come from ten, fifteen, twenty, or more miles around to trade in their stores. Once Wal-Mart came, other national and regional chains and franchises came. At first this hurt the local merchants, but now many of them have refocused their mix of goods and their approach to service and are doing well. The educational, health and governmental services have also consolidated in Agravilles, and industries have expanded to sites there.

The six-mile world of pre-World War II rural America has been replaced largely with a 30-mile to 60-mile world. (Density of population, area gross income, and location of towns of 2,500 or more are the primary reasons for variations.) Agravilles are the expression of the end product of the second wave in town and country America. For many Americans, this is the best kind of place to live. It offers many of the advantages of both urban and rural living. It is touted as an appropriate compromise of first and second wave values, and as a place where third wave lifestyles fit. No one knows how many Agravilles there are, but the number surely approaches 2,000. Many of today's seminarians will spend a significant portion of their ministry in these communities. These can be stimulating and fulfilling places of ministry.

Covington, Georgia, is an example of an Agraville. Wal-Mart is on the east end of town and K-Mart on the west. (Covington is the setting for the television series, *In the Heat of the Night, The Dukes of Hazard,* and *I'll Fly Away.*) The courthouse square has been somewhat reduced in importance, but several good stores are there still. Once, Covington was a cotton milling town with two mill villages attached, the seat of county government, and a trade center for farmers. The college town of Oxford was a nearby suburb. In a decade Covington will be an Atlanta Ribbonville, but for now, it is a strong Agraville. Several nice industries have replaced the mills as key employers. A hospital provides primary care. The consolidated high school is well respected. A concert-lyceum program brings five or six good cultural events to the community each year. For several blocks along Floyd Street, east from the square past the Baptist church, one finds more than a score of fine antebellum homes. South of the square a few blocks sits a classic Episcopalian church with a second cluster of prestigious old homes surrounding it. Like many such southern towns, Covington has a sizeable African-American community. Poor whites live in the old homes of the mill towns. It is a proud town. The mix of the old and the new results in some tensions.

Walrath and Dudley have developed a church typology that works especially well when analyzing Agravilles.[4] Generally, the town has a "dominant" congregation. Often it is the largest. Often it contains most of the power figures. Usually, it corresponds with the CMS map of denominations in the United

States. Because of the presence of Emory at Oxford, Covington deviates some from this typology in that the First Methodist, rather than First Baptist, is the premiere congregation. Often the dominant denomination in an Agraville will have a branch congregation on the outskirts of town and/or across the railroad tracks, that traditional boundary of social class. Often it exercises considerable control over community life. Sometimes a branch will become larger in membership than the mother congregation, but seldom does it become more powerful.

The second type is the "denominational" church. This is the "corral" that gathers up "our kind of folk"—the people who identify with "our" denomination. Usually, it is a relatively small, static, friendly congregation that mixes culture, ethnic or regional, with the gospel. During the first wave era of rural settlement it may have competed with the dominant church for hegemony. But now it has settled into a secondary role, and is an aging, perhaps dying, congregation. (Many mainline town and county congregations are like this.)

"Distinctive" is the label for the third type as identified by Dudley and Walrath. It may be a charismatic fellowship meeting in a metal building with a dove on its sign out on the by-pass around town. Or it may be the extension of a regional denomination that is attempting to become national. In either case, it tends to be aggressive in outreach and sees its "church field" not as three miles from its door but fifteen or twenty. The coming of these congregations to the Agravilles has resulted in growing diversity of the stock of congregations. Whereas in 1950 Covington had less than a dozen different denominations represented, it now has more than twenty five, plus several independent groups. It seems that often the new distinctive groups pick off the poorer and less committed members of the dominant and denominational congregations as well as evangelizing the unchurched. Certainly, as one observer puts it, "There are lots more hooks in the pond," today.

In some instances, one of the congregations of the dominant denomination has also redefined its church field as being thirty miles in diameter. It has stopped being limited by the old first wave parish mentality. It recognizes that with increasing diversity within its county there are people living in what were once the parishes of sister churches who are not attending there and will more likely attend the regional dominant church. This is illustrative of the fact that for many rural Americans, the *county*, centered in the Agraville, has become the new community boundary replacing the township village. Increasingly, there is not only a kind of ecology of all of the denominations in a county, but also an intra-denominational ecology—churches of the same family but with distinctive styles, activities, and foci. As in the cities, also in the country, it is becoming more common for a person to pass several congregations of her denomination on the way to the one where she worships. This rise of Agravilles with their consolidation of county life is opening a new day for rural ministry. Some are now calling this larger regional church a "Wal-Mart" church because it offers a wide variety of activities and ministries. It is a kind of rural version of the megachurch.

Different agricultures dominate particular regions. A minister in a town and country setting needs to learn about the agriculture of the area. Often it sets the rhythm of the area. Grain, cattle, or milk prices may be reflected in the collection plate. Values, concerns, lifestyle, and health can all be related to the agriculture practiced in the region. Social class, status, and power relationships are also tied to the processes of earning a living. It is beyond the scope of this text to examine each of these agricultures. This is an area of study that the student may wish to pursue on his or her own.[5]

Mighthavebeenville

The third type presented by Sim is called "Mighthavebeenville," not a flattering appellation. He uses this name to refer to the many thousands of six-mile hamlets, villages, and small towns that have fallen under the domination of the Agravilles. Many of these towns are a much shrunken version of their former selves. Saturdays were once lively on Main Street as farmers came to shop. Now they drive on through on their way to the Wal-Mart in Agraville. Once the school yard was filled with the shouts of children. Now the children are bussed twelve miles away into Agraville. Once one could call upon the village physician, and he would make a house call. But now he is part of a group practice in a clinic in Agraville. The Mighthavebeen-villes were begun with great expectations and some had years of glory. Today most are just hanging on.

The Mighthavebeenville churches are often the first pastorate out of seminary. The membership is often old and discouraged. Quite honestly, many could be renamed Little Hope Church. But a mixture of pride and guilt keeps them going. Many an urban, sophisticated, rational denominational judicatory officer has concluded that they are inefficient and should be closed. Just let her try.

On the other hand, there are other Mighthavebeenville congregations that are vital and effective and some that could be so, given the opportunity with leaders of vision and hope. Sometimes it is the only survivor of three or four other congregations that once served the community. Often there are still people around to be reached. Often these churches have shifted, consciously or by good luck, from being a denominationally oriented program church to one that intentionally serves everyone in their community in a relational way (new first wave). Some have become more inclusive. Others have opted to drop denominational affiliation. And still others have changed affiliation to more nearly parallel the preferences of the persons in their community.

The primary problem for many Mighthavebeenville congregations is "how to pay the pastor." Yoking, cooperative parishes, blending, and developing a field or circuit are among the common approaches. Some have turned to "lay" pastors or to bi-vocational arrangements. The fact is that it costs somewhere between $60,000 and $100,000 annually to "do" basic church with a fully supported minister. Many small town and country churches do not have resources to pay this. So, if they do not receive a subsidy from their denomination, or if the spouse of their pastor does not earn enough from his/her employment to support the family of their pastor, then one of these other arrangements becomes necessary. Increasingly, persons preparing for ministry in seminaries are planning to be "intentional" bivocational pastors. Given the large number of "second-career" students, this seems to be an option worthy of exploration.

A growing number of Mighthavebeenville churches are electing to become "signature" congregations. A signature church identifies a need or opportunity that is not being met presently in its thirty-mile area. It discovers resources in its body that can address this opportunity. It learns how to do an excellent job at this ministry. One example is a rural church that decided back in 1980 to put on a passion play. It had only about 125 active members. It was a success. Now 30,000 persons come for a dozen outdoor performances each season. Another is a church that decided to focus on ministry to the home schoolers in its county. Another grew out of an AA group. Another finds meaning around a prayer ministry. Another has a country gospel band that performs at a variety of area events. The list goes on and on. Some persons are drawn to these churches as a means of using their gifts and graces for God. Others come because it meets their needs. It is our thinking that these may well be the precursors of the primary form of third wave churches. This "signature ministry" may be the primary identifying feature of third wave churches. Third wave megachurches will be a collection of signature ministry groups.

Sim laments the loss and decline of Mighthavebeenville communities. So do many rural sociologists and denominational rural church officers. The fact is, however, that new community boundaries are being formed here in the latter days of the second wave. Thirty-mile communities, roughly equivalent to a county's area, are replacing six-mile ones. It appears that wisdom dictates that these Mighthavebeenville communities should come to see themselves as neighborhoods within the larger county community, because they can no longer be independent communities in themselves. The basic institutional elements are no longer there. Control of their destiny seems to have passed into other hands. The past is past. The future will not be like the present. But it is the present that is. One important task of the pastor in the Mighthavebeenville church is to aid the people in coming to terms with the present. Work for a good future. The third wave will bring new forms of community. What they will be is still open for input.

Fairview

"Fairview" is the term Sim uses to describe the growing number of rural communities whose economic base is grounded in recreational activities. Gaming, skiing, fishing, water sports, beaches, and retirement communities come to mind. Added to these might be a subcategory of "institutional" towns, those serving colleges, military bases, and prisons. This is Sim's fourth type. Typically, the Fairviews provide a service for city dwellers. They come to this rural place for a vacation, a set period of time, or for retirement. Rural residents provide services for the visitors. Myrtle Beach, Branson, Gatlinburg, Vale, and Tahoe are but a very few of hundreds of examples. As our population ages and our cities grow more violent, increasing numbers are retiring in lake, beach, or mountain communities. And growing numbers of younger persons are electing to live in town and country places and telecommute to their work in distant places. These are the early explorers of what Toffler sees as a significant portion of the third wave lifestyle. Summer homes, weekend cottages and condos, retirement villages, and upscale mobile home parks and camping facilities are becoming the badge of the middle class. Longer, as well as better financed, retirements and multiple vacations during the year are now common.

Third Wave Models

The Community Presbyterian Church in Lake City, Colorado is located in a county that is 97 percent National Forest Land. It has the lowest population of any county in the United States. The main industry in this county is tourism, and there are no social services. Fifty percent of the congregation's funds come from summer visitors, and 10 percent of the needed income comes from an endowment fund.

The ministry of this church changes dramatically throughout the year as the tourist season changes. The congregation of 25–30 from September 15 to June 15 may be absent during the summer months because they are busy dealing with the visitors who provide their yearly income. During this period of time as many as 300 attend Sunday services. These summer residents do much of the ministry—from ushering to singing to working with youth in building maintenance.

This community of Telluride, Colorado is a former mining town on the western slope of the Rockies. In recent years, it has become a popular Fairview type of community. More than 1,000 ex-urban professionals make it their primary home. Many of these "telecommute" to their jobs on the coasts. Data from marketing ("psycho-graphics") sources indicates a slightly larger number of service workers. The consequent picture is one of a bimodal community. If you were a church planting strategist, would you call for one or two congregations? Why?

Some Fairviews are reborn Mighthavebeenvilles and Agravilles. Others are almost brand new. Some like Colorado Springs have grown beyond being a Fairview and become significant cities in their own right.

Fairview churches need to address both the visitor and the long time resident. Many Fairviews are seasonal communities, so churches wax and wane. Their activities must have the flexibility of an accordion. These churches need to adjust to the schedules of their members and of their visitors. Some Fairview churches will experience difficulty in bridging the differences between the regular rural members and their irregular urban visitors.

Particularly in the retirement oriented Fairviews, there seems to be a need to plant urban churches in rural settings. Included features would be structure and decor of the building, form of worship, sensitivity to visitors, selection of music, style and syntax of the sermon, teaching methods, and the degree of formality in the worship event. Some contemporary seminarians will have the challenging experience of forming a new congregation in a Fairview. Just as village churches were brought to the emerging cities in the late nineteenth and the early twentieth centuries, urban churches will be planted in rural places at the end of the twentieth and the beginning of the twenty-first.

Because Fairviews often attract many low-pay, service industry jobs, care must be taken to design churches sensitive to this segment of the population. Some of the service workers will be local persons who may be members of area churches. Often their jobs will interfere with regular participation in the life of the congregation to which they belong. Perhaps these churches can be flexible. Perhaps new congregations targeting service workers will need to be formed. Some of the workers will be ethnics. Consideration should be given to starting churches that appeal to them and address their needs.

"The Heights of the Mountains Are His"

The Thanksgiving Day 1994 pastoral of Archbishop J. Francis Stafford addresses a situation that is emerging in a number of Fairview communities.

Titled "The Heights of the Mountains Are His: The Development of God's Country," the pastoral drew attention to the impact of rapid development, especially that of the Western Slope of the Rockies in Colorado, on its long-term inhabitants and on the ecology of the area. The consequences of well-capitalized development may be to turn local residents into low-paid service providers and to force them to relocate:

"What we risk creating, then, is a theme-park 'alternative reality' for those who have the money to purchase entrance. Around this Rocky Mountain theme park will sprawl a growing buffer zone of the working poor. In the last century the Western Slope functioned as a resource colony for timber and mining interests. Those scars will be with us for generations. We cannot afford to stand by now as the culture of a leisure colony, like the walled communities which dominate so many American suburbs, takes its place. The West is famous for its hospitality, but we are watching the warmth of a friendly handshake disappear.

All of us . . . have a stake in our common future, in using our freedom in the pursuit of justice. While the geological foundations of our state are literally set in granite, the moral foundations of our shared life, and of our care for the environment, must be rooted in conscience and purity of heart. . . .We are stewards not simply of the land, but of one another's well-being and rights. . . .

The task on the Western Slope is not to indict any particular group or shut down the tourist resorts in an effort to return to an imagined pristine past; but to encourage growth in a direction, and at a pace, and with a variety that serves the maximum number of people who actually live and work there in the best possible way. The ultimate guiding norm for any development on the Western Slope is safeguarding and promoting the transcendent dignity of the human person as the visible image of the invisible God."

Paragraphs 20 and 34 of the pastoral letter.

Characteristics of a Church for Poor People

In the first wave age of conquest of the West, many congregations seemed to target poor people. Often the second wave period found them moving away from their roots and focusing upon the upwardly mobile. Some of the poor found their way into the emerging pentecostal and holiness denominations. Again it seems to be time to target churches for the poor as we move into the era of the third wave. Tex Sample, a professor at Saint Paul School of Theology in Kansas City, has focused our attention on this need in a series of books. Drawing from his work and that of others we want to suggest about a dozen characteristics of such churches:

Loving acceptance of sinners (bad folk)

The sharing of good counsel from the Bible

Healing for physical, psychic, and spiritual maladies

Active intercessory prayer for the needs of members, their kin, and friends

Deep faith that trusting Jesus makes a difference now and hereafter

Blessings that come without merit or manipulation of God

Expressive worship

Networks of caring

Creative involvement in the life and ministry of the congregation by discovering, training, and expressing one's giftedness

Growth of the body both by inclusion and by extension

Personal spiritual development

Raising up and mentoring the indigenous leaders

As with any typology there are town and country communities which do not fit neatly into one of these categories. But most seem to do so. Each of the four types has unique challenges and opportunities. Each has a specific set of churches that it needs. We hope that this discussion has been helpful in making you more aware of the diversity of rural communities and churches. Much too often people have stereotypical views of rural church and community life that are not only incorrect, but that also set them up for failure. Understanding the complexity of rural communities, especially the specific nature of one's own, can point in helpful directions.

Rural ministry in this hinge-time will not be easy. It calls for persons with creative, entrepreneurial skills. Ministry in each of the four types of communities will be different. Of particular importance for many Mighthavebeenville churches will be to refocus their ministry from being a six-mile community church to being a church with a signature ministry in a thirty-mile community. Many Agraville churches will want to consider becoming mini-megachurches for their 30-mile community. Some Ribbonville and Fairview churches will want to look at becoming urbane in style and focus. Undoubtedly, some major surprises await us. And some unanticipated consequences will appear—good and bad.

While Sim's typology provides a help in understanding the diversity of rural communities at the end of the second wave era, one also needs some handles for understanding the specific context in which he/she will be serving. The list of topics provided in the "Thirty Questions to Answer Concerning a Rural Community" (Appendix A) has been widely used in training pastors new to a rural setting in how to learn about their context. Draw upon it in discovering the life and culture of your place of ministry.

Most churches are found in non-metro places. So, it is probable that many, if not most, present day seminarians will spend at least a portion of their ministry in one of these places. It seems to be generally held that now is a time of major paradigmatic shift. Town and country leaders and pastors must come to grips with the end of the second wave era as it is being played out, often painfully, in their place, but they must also be preparing for the arrival of the third wave. Change is the order of the day. Communities and churches must respond. But effective response to the second wave may not be adequate for the third and vice versa. We believe that the third wave can be a time of renewal and vitality in the rural United States. Whether or not it is depends upon how congregations respond to issues that are emerging there.

The typologies of Toffler and of Sim help us understand rural church and community life. We focus now on how the third wave will impact rural America and consider how rural churches might ride this wave to address real opportunities for mission, ministry, and evangelism. We want to invite you to share with us ways in which you unpack the implications of the third wave in your ministry setting. (Please direct your material to the Center for Theology and Land, 2000 University Avenue, Dubuque, IA 52001, for possible use in later editions.)

The Third Wave and the Rural Church

Toffler and others identify this with the Information Age.[6] Transferring information will become an important industry. Jobs and place of residence will be further de-coupled and then re-coupled in new ways. Toffler, Naisbitt, and others envision a time when increasing numbers of persons will live in Fairviews and Agravilles and commute to work via computers. Networking with colleagues across the nation and the globe will be common. Limiting one's accessibility (cocooning), re-training several times during one's working life, avocational activities, cottage industries, and the economic bifurcation of society are among the commonly cited consequences.

It seems very likely that the unique third wave churches will appear first in the Fairviews. These will be urban churches in rural settings. They will address the needs of telecommuting professionals and draw upon their skills and resources. Many will be focused on very specific missional ministries that will network around the globe. Cutting-edge technological ways of sharing the gospel and meeting needs will be formulated, put into perspective, and shared widely. Lay persons will do the work of the church as never before.

Now deep in the second wave and beginning to experience the third wave, it appears that added to the "parish" and the "program" churches will be a third type—the mission/ministry "project" church. The "draw" of this congregation will be the type of persons it focuses upon and the work it does to advance the kingdom of God in the world. Mead, Callahan and others are calling the church to be "on mission."[7] Many are responding. Others are being newly formed around a particular mission. These will be different from the parish church and from the program church. Their participants will come because the church is offering a ministry they need, or one that they want to assist in offering. Some who come seeking ministry will find it, stay, and become ministry providers. Examples of such ministries for third wave congregations include vocationally-based Bible study, lifestyle and life-stage support groupings, family development, and vocationally-based ministries. The ministry will not be a standard product from the denomination. Rather it will be a creative, contextualized ministry for which the ministers are gifted. In a given region a very diverse set of ministries will emerge. Anyone will be able to find a congregation which she or he fits. If not, then one might be started.

If this is correct, profound impacts upon town and country churches and communities can be anticipated. Leonard Sweet suggests many of these in *FaithQuakes*.[8]

Some Quotes from *Faithquakes* Related to Rural Church and Community

No longer can we expect people to fit into the church's rhythms, rhythms that reflect the lost paradise of rurality and the agriculturally-based economy of early twentieth century village life. The rhythms of people's lives today don't match the "rurbanity" rhythm of the church's life. (pages 27–28)

91

What if the church were to provide the people with the kind of intimacy that family offers—place where people laugh and cry together, look out for one another, take care of their weakest members? What if the church took seriously Jesus' mandate to care for the marginalized, the disenfranchised? (page 31)

The key number of meta-church is ten, although even smaller numbers like four (holy club) and five (haystack prayer meeting) have had great effect. The cutting edge of missionary churches is double-edged: more mega church and more micro/alternative church. (page 75)

The church must help post-moderns restore faith in simple pleasures, simple relationships, simple loyalties—what the Stanford Research Institutes calls "living in a way that is outwardly simple and inwardly rich." (page 78)

Small towns and small town churches must be prepared to change, especially to become more "small town," if they are to benefit from the urb exodus. The church can also help small towns get themselves to withstand the pressure from newly arrived urban romantics to transform rural towns into neo-suburbs with wider highways, paved roads, more fast food outlets, and so on. (page 138)

The driving force of the church must be the "laity," not the "clergy." If a community is to be in mission and ministry, it needs a variety of leaders making a variety of contributions and offering a variety of gifts. No clerical offices or ordination rites were asserted in the early church. (page 142)

Not too long ago, an average worker spent an average of 100,000 hours or 50 years on the job. It will soon be just 50,000 hours or 25 years on a "job." What will people at their creative working peaks do with that 50,000 hours? Use the stability, experience, and knowledge selfishly, sitting out a third of their lives in retirement centers or motor homes? Or use it to the glory of God—learning new skills and developing parts of themselves so that they can leave this world better than they found it? (pages 154–55)

> People are now spending an average of 23 years in retirement. Unprecedented! According to an Ohio University psychologist, everyone's best chances of having an annual income of $1 million dollars or more will arrive when we're between 80 and 89 years old. (page 154)
>
> The forces of integration and disintegration operate in tandem; we are becoming more and more "world citizens" and "tribal citizens" all at the same time; the world is becoming more "at home" and "abroad" at once. (page 180)
>
> The institutional church must become a missional and connectional church. (page 185)
>
> Because God is absolute, it is not true that there are no better or worse answers. Because God is absolute, it is not true that all answers have the same weight, that it's all "a matter of opinion." Because God is absolute, there are standards; there are canons; there are wrong answers. It is time the church stuck its neck out and announced that some ways of living are better than others. It is time that Christians started showing people how to make value judgements again. Postmodern Christians must not give up on the idea of Truth. (page 190)
>
> It is important for the church to understand that the environment is not just another social justice issue. Planet earth is the playing field on which all other social justice issues stand or fall. (page 195)

Mull over what Sweet is saying. What are its implications for old rural churches? for new rural churches? for your church?

Some very cosmopolitan churches will be needed in many rural places. Ministry to the poor will become even more needed. In many instances place has become less important than lifestyle interests as a focus for community life. Choices about whom to relate to will not be determined by location. Many see the third wave church as focused on ministry. It will call upon believers to employ their technological knowledge to provide ministry to others. Projects will join program and place as organizing principles for church life. Imagine a fellowship of engineers and construction workers developing good, affordable housing for the poor as an expression of their Christianity, while sharing their faith with their colleagues and those to whom they minister. Imagine a fellowship of health care professionals developing a free clinic in a rural ghetto, healing, evangelizing, and giving hope. Imagine a fellowship of agriculturalists training the poor in how to earn a living on a small plot of ground by practicing intensive, but sustainable agriculture, sharing their commitment to Jesus as Savior. Imagine the poor modeling their faith as they serve the needs of the wealthy. Imagine both coming together around efforts to create a more just society, one made possible by new technology that both produces enough for all and frees the majority for doing good one to the other.

Consider starting a third wave congregation. It may be one that meets in the facilities of the first or second wave congregation where you now belong. What role might you play? What people group(s) are to be found within twenty or thirty minutes of your church that are not being reached well by anyone? Contact them and ask them what they would want in a church that they might attend. This may include concerns about program, place, time of meeting, dress code, music, worship style, ministry activities etc. For ideas about a ministry based church you might begin with a review of books such as R. Coote, *Mustard-seed Churches* (Fortress Press), R. Sider, *Cup of Water, Bread of Life* (Zondervan), and C. Dudley, *Basic Steps Toward Community Ministry* (Alban Institute).

Not everyone shares our hope of a bright future for town and county U.S. Some futurists like the Poppers and Alan Bird look at portions of rural America and see it as even more depopulated.[9] The Poppers have suggested that the Great Plains be given back to the buffaloes. Bird sees a day when farmers will live in cities and commute by aircraft to the Great Plains to sow and reap their crops. Others like Wendell Berry and Wes

Jackson call for a resettling of rural America with "more eyes to the acre." They want to recapture elements of the first wave community while recognizing that society cannot go back.[10] Often they sound like "Agrarian Fundamentalists" and their antagonists like "Modernists." There is an irony here. For the agrarian fundamentals are usually more liberal in theology than their modernist foes. This is to say that even many who are fundamentalist in theology are modernist in their acceptance of modern technology, and vice versa.

CHAPTER FIVE

Emerging Issues in Rural America

"When I lost my farm, I *knew* that God loved me, that Christ died for me, and that the church is Christ's body here on earth, but I didn't *feel* any of that," said a bivocational Iowa pastor.

*   *   *

The Hispanic pastor of a church in one of California's Central Valley towns known to some as "cancer-cluster communities" said: "The planes regularly spray the fields of the valley with pesticides and sometimes the spray drifts to the playground of our school. Why aren't the authorities more interested in the extraordinarily high number of our children who have a variety of horrible diseases like lupus and cancer?"

*   *   *

"They lost their farms in the Midwest," said a Wyoming social worker, "and they came here to work in the oil fields. Things have gone bust here now also and they have no money to get back home to their families, wherever home is."

*   *   *

"My largely rural state," said a North Carolina church leader, "has both the lowest rate of *un*employment in the nation *and* one of the highest rates of poverty."

Out of the many and diverse voices of rural America, the shape of issues with which the church *and* society must deal begins to emerge. While there are many counties whose futures seem bright, as the previous two chapters have noted, there are many others whose futures are at best ambiguous, as the quotations above indicate. This chapter undertakes the task of locating the trends that are impacting rural communities.

From the Atlantic to the Pacific, from the Arctic Ocean to the Gulf of Mexico, within each state and every county therein, rural peoples live in richly different cultural and physical settings. In the face of such diversity, it is nearly impossible to even mention all the issues that confront people. Yet we are convinced that to be in ministry in rural areas without some understanding of the implications of these issues is a prescription for a less than fully effective ministry.

The "big picture" issues we will discuss seem to be mainly economic with significant social, psychological, and political content; however, every one of them has spiritual and justice aspects as well, aspects that we will address in subsequent chapters. Every one of these issues in subtle and not so subtle ways is changing the way rural people function in their individual and community lives.

Three important points must be made at the outset. The first is that many of these issues are not newly emerging ones. They "emerged" as important concerns some years ago but continue to affect rural life in significant ways. Second, these issues affect all of American society, urban and rural, directly and/or indirectly. Most of them have implications for communities around the globe. But in rural America we see them played out "up close and personal." We often know by name and place families and communities affected by them and thus we are unable to deny the consequences of these issues. Third, almost all of them raise significant moral dilemmas for Christians, dilemmas that are frequently too threatening to discuss even within the body of Christ. We lift them up here because we believe that the church must name them and confront them in order to deal with rural America in an honest, community-enhancing way. To ignore or deny what is happening and to fail to take action to bring positive change, even while caring for those suffering the consequences, would be to disregard our calling to be God's people of justice and of compassion.

The Changing Nature of the Rural Economy

Change never occurs in a vacuum, but always in context. To comprehend how significant the changes now occurring in rural society are, one must have at least some sense of the historical context in which they are grounded.

A Look Backward **The European settlers who landed on the eastern shores of the North American continent learned much from the indigenous peoples about living on the land. They formed agriculturally based colonies which for several decades supplied raw materials for shipment back to Europe for processing before some returned as finished goods for the people of the colonies to buy. In time, colonial status was traded for nationhood. The Industrial Revolution came to our continent and a growing nation began to make use of developing technologies and responded to the needs of an expanding, industrializing country.**

The family-owned and operated farm, ranch, and local business became the norm in most regions of the country as an eager, pioneering population moved to fill in the open spaces between the coasts.[1] Technology, of course, dramatically and constantly changed nearly every aspect of the way food and fiber, products and services, were produced and transported. However, for the most part, the structure of much of the agricultural and small business segments of the expanding rural economy remained very much centered in family units until well into the post-World War II years of the 1950s.

The major sectors of the rural economy were no strangers to boom and bust cycles. Mining communities developed quickly and vanished almost overnight when the coal seam or the ore ran out. The 1920s and 30s witnessed many families losing their farms and rural businesses in the Great Depression and the years of the Dust Bowl that followed.

From Sod House to Cyberspace

The incredible pace of technological change that has so altered rural America can be illustrated succinctly in my own family. In 1909, my father-in-law was born in a sod house on the South Dakota Prairie to parents who were trying unsuccessfully to homestead a quarter section of land. The family soon returned to Iowa.

Following graduation from high school, Dad worked in a tractor factory to accumulate enough money for him and Mom to start a small family farming operation in the late 1930s. They began with horses for draft power and retired in the late 1970s with the biggest four-wheel drive tractor that John Deere made. When Dad died in 1993, our 23 year old daughter drove with us to her grandfather's memorial service editing a writing project on her battery-powered laptop computer. From sod house to cyberspace within the lifetime of one man!

As told by Judith Bortner Heffernan

The Second World War brought some measure of recovery to the rural economy. The GI Bill helped many returning veterans get an education, and with confidence, some returned to ranching or farming. But difficult days of low prices followed in the 1950s and 60s. During the 1970s, however, several international and domestic factors combined to increase the income and optimism of U.S. farmers. Farm magazines predicted that the 1980s would be the "Golden Age of American Agriculture."

The 1980s and the Rural Crisis They were wrong. The relatively good commodity prices of the 1970s came to a screeching halt as the world economic picture underwent significant changes that led to a major decline in U.S. farm exports and in farm incomes. Government policies to control inflation led to the doubling of real interest rates, which drove land prices in rural America down to as low as one-third of their previous value. Almost overnight, farms and rural businesses that depended on borrowed money to operate were thrown into deep financial trouble. The "farm crisis" had begun.

Across the country, farm bankruptcies mushroomed. Families stood on courthouse steps and watched their farms sold at auction, farms that in some cases their grandparents had homesteaded. Financially unable to save their own farms, many farmers were incapable of repaying their bankers, equipment dealers, and other persons with whom they had done business on credit. When many of these enterprises were forced out of business, the "farm crisis" became the "rural crisis." The cycle escalated when urban manufacturing workers were laid off due to the fact that farmers stopped buying new machinery, equipment, and vehicles. By October of 1986 the American Banking Association had identified 20 states in which over 50 families *per week* were losing their land.[2]

Something over 600,000 farm families lost their land in the 1980s. A Native American friend of a displaced Nebraska farm woman compassionately, but profoundly, remarked, "Now you too know how it feels to be unwillingly and forcefully removed from your land."

So extensive was this displacement in the rural U.S. and later in Canada that few congregations or communities were left untouched. Disbelief and denial about what was happening soon gave way to depression and despair. The number of suicides among farmers surpassed all other occupational groups in the states that kept vital statistics by occupation. Initially, pastors and congregations were at a loss about how to respond to the profound levels of depression and hopelessness that accompanied such extensive economic loss.[3]

Although the couples told the researchers that they enjoyed a fair amount of support from family, neighbors, and close friends, they also told of feeling more condemnation and less support from their church than they felt they received from the lender that had foreclosed on them. Comments during the interviews indicated a lack of active involvement of their pastor with them over the many months of their ordeal and the failure, at least early in the crisis, of the church to speak out about what was happening to rural people.

As documentation of the deepening crisis was spread by the media and as prominent farmers known to be outstanding producers lost their land, the scope of the crisis could no longer be denied by leaders of the government, the economy, or the church. In states where Councils of Churches or similar entities existed, they often became the initiators and coordinators of a response to the crisis. Food banks were established in rural churches and community centers. Hot-lines were set up in many states to answer calls twenty four hours a day.[4]

Many who worked with hurting rural families in the 1980s and even today know that lives have literally been saved by caring, broad-based ministry. One despairing farmer, after attending an interfaith training workshop for caregivers, confessed to his wife that he had about given up and intended to end his own life. "However," he said, "if the church is going to stand with us, then I will keep going." He did and he became a powerful voice for support of other rural families and for social and economic justice.

The discussion of the rural crisis of the 1980s is included here for two major reasons beyond just historical importance. The first is that the economic situation in the agricultural and natural resource sectors of rural America today differs little from the period that came to be called the "rural crisis." Second, while it will be years before we can fully document the impact that living through this experience has had on the people most affected by it, we can gain some insight from those who lived through previous periods of massive rural disruption in the 1920s and 30s.[5] An unpublished study of college students who were between eight and eighteen years old when their families lost their farms or rural businesses in the 1980s suggests that the psychological and emotional impact of their experience may well color their lives in ways similar to that reported by the older generation.[6]

No one who experienced the rural crisis personally came away unaffected or unchanged.[7] Previously held beliefs about the value of sacrifice and hard work, the importance of the "family farm" system of agriculture, the economic security of one's children, the role of government and powerful economic institutions, the existence of the "American Dream," the future of their way of life—all of these beliefs and many others were called into question. Some individuals, as we will discuss later in the chapter, chose then and choose now to interpret their experience through the ideologies and conspiracy theories of radical hate and fear groups that feed on despair. When this context was combined with the other major changes that were occurring in rural America, the stage was set for even more family and community disruption.[8] Indeed, it is happening.

The Consequences of the Changing Structure of Agriculture "Once upon a time," only a decade or so ago, most agricultural production in North America was characterized by family-owned and operated farms and ranches, orchards and feedlots. Typically these units bought their inputs (the supplies they needed for production) in their local or a neighboring community from a supplier that was likely also a local family-owned and operated businesses. When the crops or the livestock were ready to be sold, the farm family usually marketed them through local buyers and markets, or perhaps a regional cooperative. Local suppliers, local commodity and livestock buyers most certainly sold a major portion of the production beyond the local community; however, both groups of business persons operated with a clear commitment to the welfare of the local community within which they and their customers lived.

In this "once upon a time" world of only a decade or two ago, the farmers and ranchers and the suppliers and marketers of farm products and their families all had a major stake in the future of the community in which they lived—in its physical environment, its social institutions and organizations, its economic development, its social life, and its moral and ethical climate. It was understood that shopping locally, volunteering for community service, serving in a variety of leadership roles, and supporting the betterment of the whole community were ways one could further enhance the development of a "great place to raise your kids" kind of community. Building one's community was seen as more than a civic or patriotic or even religious duty; it was also understood to make good economic sense. No wonder that national polls taken over many years continue to show that a majority of Americans say they would prefer to live in a community of 10,000 or fewer, if it were economically possible for them to do so.

The competitive, decentralized, "family farm" system of agricultural production just described and the accompanying extensive network of local businesses that symbiotically related to it became the envy of much of the world. Surplus, not scarcity, was the "problem" with which U.S. agricultural and governmental policy had to deal. And while wide swings in annual farm income, along with other concerns, have shown that the system by no means functioned perfectly, it did provide a steady, secure, safe, and abundant supply of food and fiber for this country and for those overseas who could either buy our exported commodities or were eligible for a food assistance program.

Why then are we using the past tense to describe arguably the most consistently productive system of agricultural production known in human history? The answer is at once both simple and complex. The family farm system is not dying. Rather, some suggest that "it is being killed" by governmental policies and corporate decisions that have facilitated and promoted the ascendancy of a significantly different production and marketing system, one that is highly concentrated and vertically and horizontally integrated. In a relatively short

period of time, a centralized, monopolistic, corporate-control-
led system has begun to dominate the marketing and processing
of major crops and livestock, and even the production sector
of some livestock. There is growing evidence that even the
production of major crops will soon be under such control as
well. The control of the production and processing of most of
the nation's food has become concentrated in the hands of a
few primarily transnational corporations (TNC's) that are
rapidly globalizing the world's food system.[9]

The differences between these two kinds of food systems
are stark. The consequences, both the intended and the unin-
tended ones, that changing to this globalized system is having
for rural families and their communities can hardly be overstated. The consequences for all people, rural and urban,
producers and consumers, as well as for the natural and political environments, both here and around the world, are quite
profound.

Two factors in this ongoing restructuring of the food system
are frequently referred to as "vertical and horizontal integration." Vertical integration occurs in any commodity when a
firm manufactures and/or sells most of the inputs needed to
produce a crop or livestock, and then maintains control over
the production, marketing, and processing of that commodity
and sells it as a brand name product in the supermarket. The
firm controls the system from "seed to shelf." ConAgra and
Cargill are two examples of firms involved in vertical integration on a national and international scale. They control major
portions of the system, from the fertilizers, chemicals, and seed,
to the storage, shipping, and milling of the grain, to livestock
processing and sales that occur under such brand names as
Healthy Choice meals, Banquet TV Dinners, and Country
Pride chickens.

Horizontal integration occurs when the same firms expand
in any given sector of the food system, such as grain milling,
poultry or beef processing. Three or four firms, most often
TNC's, now control between forty and eighty percent of the

slaughtering, killing, processing, and shipping of most grains and livestock in the U.S. For the most part, the **same** firms that dominate the U.S. food system control major portions of the system that moves food products in the international arena. While farm families are struggling to survive on an average of three to four percent return on their investment, the food firms expect to receive twenty percent, and often make even more.

Names of Largest Four Firms and Percentage of Market Share They Control

Broilers:

**Largest four control
46 percent of production**
Tyson
ConAgra
Gold Kist
Perdue Farms

Beef:

**Largest four control
72 percent of slaughter**
IBP
ConAgra
Cargill
Beef America

Pork Slaughter:

**Largest four control
45 percent of pork slaughter**
IBP
ConAgra
Cargill (Excel)
Sara Lee

Flour Milling:

**Largest four control
71 percent of milling**
ConAgra
Archer Daniels Midland
Cargill
General Mills

Dry Corn Milling:	Largest four control 57 percent of the milling
	Bunge
	Illinois Cereal Mills
	Archer Daniels Midland
	ConAgra (Lincoln Grain)
Source: *Catholic Rural Life*, Spring 1996, p.15	

Most consumers have little or no idea about the changes that have taken place in the production and processing of their food. The supermarkets are fully stocked, and the presence of endless brand names successfully conceals the fact that a few giant firms own and control most of these products.

Many farmers have only recently begun to fully understand the consequences of what these changes mean. Focusing on the immediate demands of their own operations, many have not had sufficient information to comprehend "the big picture." They are well aware that they operate on small margins of profit and low returns on their investment. They know they have fewer farm suppliers from which to purchase inputs and almost nothing that resembles a competitive market through which to sell their grain and livestock. Only recently have they begun to understand that changes in the whole system are transforming them from independent producers into piece rate growers, from entrepreneurs into farm "factory workers," from individuals and families who had some authentic control over their agricultural enterprises and financial well-being into small, replaceable parts of a globalizing agricultural system.

For rural communities, these changes become increasingly obvious. The impact of the corporate concentration of agriculture in a dozen major slaughtering-packing-distribution conglomerates has accompanied the global "free-trade" movements legislated by the GATT and NAFTA. The effect has been to create a sector of rural counties—specifically, those which are dependent on agriculture or other extractive industries—which continue to be in chronic decline. Some, in fact, are speaking of a "new peasant class" in rural America.

Farmers, along with the rural localities that are agriculturally dependent, are caught in a double bind. They are put at a disadvantage by farm policies that continue to be tilted in favor of large producers and that have come to enjoy the benefits of tax easement incentives and rural economic development enticements. At the same time they have, through the globalization of transnational players in the food supply system, been brought into competition with other farmers worldwide. In this they are no different from many factory and service workers, be they rural or urban. There are reports, for example, that hourly wages are at their lowest point in twenty years. And indeed many of those factory workers are rural as manufacturing firms have found that Iowans or Montanans or Georgians will work cheap.[10]

Many of these counties are those that are experiencing the "rural crisis" in a chronic way. They manifest the continuing problems of lack of employment opportunities or of good employment opportunities; poor housing; high poverty rates; relatively high illiteracy and low levels of education. These may be accompanied by lack of development skills within the local governments; a general lack of institutional and organizational infrastructure; and a lack of access to credit.[11]

These persistent trends apply with especial force to those towns and rural areas we labeled Agravilles and Mighthavebeenvilles in the previous chapter. We certainly do not want to obscure the reality that there are many rural locations where living standards have declined; in fact the depth of poverty and its attendant stress are still undocumented. There are very real costs attached to what is happening in these locations—social, family, spiritual, and emotional suffering often accompany economic loss. The church and society need to address the inequities that have produced these counties' situation.

There is another rural reality emerging, however, which is much brighter and calls on the church to develop very different ways of addressing people there. These correspond to the Ribbonvilles and Fairviews described in Chapter Four. In these, there are real opportunities for evangelism, church growth, and outreach. The rural communities whose futures look so different reflect the need for different forms of Christian discipleship. Both are challenges—one to faithfulness and growth in building just communities in the midst of formidable resistance; the other to faithful boldness and growth in calling the comfortable to share and grow in Christian stewardship.

One way of describing these two quite different rural communities is by looking at population trends. The trends we are describing depend on Census data that is just now being released and also on predictions about the impact of the "Freedom to Farm" 1995 Farm Bill.

Population Trends in Rural America

It seems clear that there will continue to be population shifts with people moving from one type of urban, rural, or suburban county to others. What has been happening in rural America over the past six or seven years, however, is quite striking. Most significantly, this story will signal the possible emergence of a "new rural" in addition to "old rural" town and country locations.

The decade of the 1980s saw a massive shift of population from the countryside ("nonmetropolitan areas" in the jargon of the Census Bureau) to the cities. Only two states actually lost population during that decade—Iowa lost 137,000 people and North Dakota lost 14,000; others in the Great Plains region gained only slightly—Illinois gained .1 percent. Metropolitan counties grew at almost four times the rate of nonmetropolitan counties.[12]

Accompanying the farm crisis of that decade, the decline of population in rural communities was interpreted as the continuation of long-term population trends with people moving from country to city that had been happening since 1920.

108

That trend was interrupted during the 1970s when the direction of migration shifted toward nonmetro areas. Nonmetro counties actually grew faster than metro counties during the decade.

Interpreting the latest Census data, Johnson and Beale discovered that the 1990s are experiencing another reversal, similar to that of the 1970s. They write that "The revival of growth in rural America is one of the biggest demographic stories of the 1990s. Three in four nonmetropolitan counties gained population between 1990 and 1994, a stunning reversal following a decade of rural decline. Now the pace of rural growth seems to be accelerating, and the implications for business are substantial."[13]

Obviously, not all nonmetro counties are growing; specifically, "The farming- and mining-dependent counties that represent the bulk of the traditional rural extractive industry areas had the least growth during 1990–94 (2.3 and 2.1 percent, respectively)."[14] It is interesting to note that the growth, even in counties that are "traditional rural extractive industry areas," is not coming from natural increase (the number of births exceeding deaths) but from migration into rural areas. The current growth spurt, hypothesize Johnson and Beale, "is rooted in long-term economic changes that favor nonmetro areas, along with the strong conviction of many Americans that small-town life is better than big-city life. Nonmetro counties also grew rapidly in the 1970s for many of the same reasons,"[15] and they mention specifically the desire to avoid many of the social problems that plague our cities. Many people view rural life as a refuge from the harriedness, the crime, the violence of urban life.

There are a number of nonmetro counties that are experiencing rapid growth; specifically, those "edge cities" that have developed commercial and employment centers at the outer boundaries of metro areas; 84 percent of these gained population between 1990 and 1994. Many rural counties are designated retirement destinations; of counties so designated 99 percent gained population. Lesser, but still impressive, gains were made by counties where the economy is based on recreation (92 percent); those that depend on manufacturing and government jobs (88 percent and 87 percent, respectively); counties where much of the land is federally owned (94 percent); counties where a great many people commute (86 percent); those whose economy is based on service-sector jobs (84 percent); and those where there is much dependence on "federal transfers" such as Social Security (75 percent). The fastest-growing nonmetro counties are located in the Mountain West, the Upper Great Lakes, the Ozarks, parts of the South, and rural areas in the Northeast.

By way of contrast, the nonmetro counties least likely to grow are those where the economy is based on the traditional rural extractive enterprises. Of these only 47 percent are growing. These are farming and mining counties by and large. Johnson and Beale point out, however, that even here, growth is more widespread than in the 1980s. (As best we can project, the Freedom to Farm Act will have the effect of reducing the number of full-time farmers even further.) The poorest and most remote counties in the U.S. are not experiencing much inmigration—70 percent of them are growing but only 53 percent are gaining migrants. Finally, only 55 percent of the "low-density counties" are growing. The nonmetro counties that are still losing population in the 1990s are concentrated in the Great Plains, Western Corn Belt, and Mississippi Delta.[16]

How are we to make sense of this data? In some ways what is happening in rural America reflects what is happening throughout the society. Dr. Ray Marshall, former Secretary of Labor, in remarks made at the National Rural Development Consultation in March 1996 suggested that there is a significant gap in the distribution of income today; i.e., the most wealthy in our society are better off than they have been, the bottom 80% is not as well off. The greatest impact is at the bottom of the income pyramid. His image is that we have gone from an economy that had a diamond-shaped income distribution to one that has an hourglass configuration. In short, the middle class (which used to include family farmers and miners) is emptying out.

Our clear impression from the Census data and the changing income distribution structure is that there are two very different types of rural areas today. First there is the county where the traditional rural industries continue to be either in decline or doing less well than they used to. This is the county we have been focusing on in this chapter to this point and which we have referred to earlier as Agravilles and Mighthavebeen-villes. We believe that the witness of the church and the leadership of rural congregations can be sources of great spiritual and social strength that enable communities to follow God's will for human and ecological flourishing. They can call their communities to justice.

But there is another rural out there that has a less challenging row to hoe, at least in one way. There are counties which are growing rapidly that contain Ribbonvilles and Fairviews; in those counties there are many capable and wealthy people moving in. There are opportunities for the church to grow in religious fervor, virtue, and numbers. The challenge in these rural counties will be to practice the evangelism of calling people into community with Jesus Christ and their neighbors. If the migrants into these counties exhibit a tendency to seek out pastoral rural towns to escape the demands of urban problems, and if they are reluctant to seek out community relations with others there, the church will have its hands full in calling them to evangelism and mission for the sake of others.

Trends Affecting Community Services

Some rural communities have ceased to be the center of services for their counties. Neither do towns and localities serve as profit centers for their counties but have instead become profit centers for others. Similarly, the only input that many rural peoples still have in the local economy is their labor. It is important to think about how these communities could once again become profit centers; first steps include buying locally, joining community supported agriculture ventures; returning to local self-sufficiency; and encouraging simple community-oriented relationships and opportunities to interact with each other.

At present, however, these communities have lost hospitals and immediate access to medical services; local banks march to the directives of distant policy-makers; schools have been consolidated. There may be fewer services available than there were formerly. Part of the reason for this—and the reason we have spent so much time dwelling on population trends—is that there are fewer people in many traditionally rural counties. It is simply assumed that with more rapid transportation and higher technology, services can be accessed from any place in little time. In some ways the computer and related technology have seemed to render place and distance irrelevant.

There are fewer people but another factor seems to be that there are now larger farming operations that may not be worked by the people who own them. The size of the average farm has increased from 297 acres in 1960 to 374 acres in 1970 to 478 acres in 1994.[17] In the 1940s Dr. Walter Goldschmidt sought to document the way that land tenure and farm size affect the quality of community life in rural towns ("the Arvin and Dinuba study"). What Goldschmidt discovered in his classic study, which has been replicated many times over with similar conclusions, was that in those communities with smaller operations that were worked by their owners there were many more voluntary associations—Boy Scouts, Rotary, church groups, public school support groups, etc.—and a higher quality of life. As farm size and absentee ownership increase, social conditions in the local community deteriorate.[18]

Farms by Size and Value of Sales		
	1992	**1987**
Number of Farms	1,925,300	2,087,759
1 to 9 acres:	166,496	183,257
10 to 49 acres:	387,711	412,437
50 to 179 acres:	584,146	644,849
180 to 499 acres:	427,648	478,294
500 to 999 acres:	186,387	200,058
1,000 or more:	172,912	168,865
Farms by Value Of Sales:		
Less than $2,500	422,767	490,296
$2,500 to $49,999	195,354	219,636
$50,000 to $99,999	187,760	218,050
$100,000 or more	333,865	295,721

Source: *Catholic Rural Life,* quoting the 1992 Census of Agriculture

There is a vicious circle in operation here. With the loss of the communities' character as profit centers, many of the rewards for initiative and entrepreneurial drive were eliminated. Poverty among rural families and rural communities is increasing. Furthermore, and the long-term significance of this cannot be overestimated, the amount of time that families spend working several jobs is escalating. Only 17 percent of farm income comes from farming operations these days. Eighty-three percent comes from second or third jobs. People are driving greater distances to work. In short, a very real squeeze is being placed on the family's time. The community consequences of these dynamics are phenomenal. It is difficult to find capable people to guide the local church council or session, to offer time as Girl Scout leaders, to carry on the many voluntary associations that have been the backbone of the quality of rural life and the democratic tradition.

What has also become clear is that rural poverty is growing. In its August 8, 1988, issue *Newsweek* reported that the rate of poverty in rural areas had matched or exceeded that in central city neighborhoods. That has continued. Many of the people who have moved into rural America are the new poor, the welfare poor, the people that mainline churches have difficulty attracting. There is some influx of the urban poor who have heard that housing is dirt cheap in rural America. There is some promise that one's money will go farther, the kids will be safer, but often those kids do not receive the sort of care that they deserve when parents have to work part time at several jobs or commute long distances. The families are much more mobile; they are less secure tenants; and they frequently get little support from extended families. Rural poverty is an issue that just keeps on reverberating.

The impact of these losses on families includes stress, depression, alcoholism, and abuse. Pastors and mental health professionals who may start out defining this as an "economic restructuring" quickly see that it is a psychological, social, and spiritual crisis as well. Individual levels of depression are high. Collective depression settles over communities. Services and community networks are overloaded. Psychological consequences include withdrawal, a sense of worthlessness, sleep disorders, restlessness, increased fear, violence, abuse, mood changes, confusions, and suicide. Many rural families feel out of control. Decisions are made by people a great social distance away from rural life. There are fewer services and they are harder to access in rural America; families feel as though they have few allies to help them respond to destabilizing problems.

The nature of jobs in the countryside is changing. There are minimum wage jobs with few or no benefits to be had, and a woman or man may have to drive some distance to get them. The minimum wage is $4.65 as of this writing; translated into a full time income, that comes to $9300 a year, hardly enough to raise a family, and still some $4000 less than the federally set poverty income for a family of four. In this situation both husband and wife work, many in addition to farming, and sometimes one or both work two jobs. In short, a major sector of rural Americans in some locations are fully employed, but still have difficulty realizing a decent standard of living. Clearly this leaves little time for raising a family or community activities.

Major Changes in Rural Poverty [19]

EARLY 1970s	EARLY 1990s
Predominantly in isolated pockets of poverty	Small towns and trailer parks as well as isolated places
Multi-generational poverty	"New" poverty as well as "old"
Local people	Local people and newcomers from urban areas
Stable residence	More uprooted and mobile
Ownership of homes	Insecure tenancy
Commitment to marriage and nuclear family	Weakening marriage, unstable, family, single parenthood
Reliance on extended family and friends for support	Support from relatives and friends less accessible or effective
Economic strategies to minimize cash needs	Increased cash needs that exceed available resources
Jobs low-level, but stable, strong commitment to work	Employment deterioration—wages, benefits, security, commitment
Independence, coping strategies to "make-do on our own"	Less able to cope on own, desire for "independence"

It also impacts the style of ministry for pastors of rural churches. How can the church stand with these hard-working people without expecting them to become contributing members of our church organizations? Mainline Protestant churches are working to discover ways of appealing to and assisting people who work this hard, and whose resources render them vulnerable to many contingencies—e.g., the car breaking down, or kids getting sick. Clergy may also have the impression that landowners are wealthy due simply to the fact that they own land. However, owning land can disguise the fact that a family's situation is marginal or that most of a farmer's assets are tied up in land and loans. Pastors may feel that church members could put more in the collection plate and that their salaries could be increased by such landowners. In other words, there may be some real conflict in the church if it is under pressure to raise the pastor's salary, when members feel that their own situations are stretching them to pay what the pastor now receives.

Diversity, Racism, and Violence in Rural America

Gone are the days when rural America was immune from the social problems that afflict urban centers. Indeed, as we have noted, there is considerable inmigration from cities, and rural communities have bred their own practices that are destructive to body and soul. Let us mention alcoholism and family abuse, which have long been issues in rural America.

There is, however, a new diversity in rural America. Besides traditional white families of European—usually Northern European—ancestry, there are now a considerable number of Hispanic and Asian workers who are brought into meat packing operations from outside the region. There is also a growing diversity of income groups represented in rural America; in addition to the middle class, which may be slipping into working and poverty class incomes, there are families on welfare, there are also many "landed aristocracy" who have done very well by rural industry and investments, and there are many retirees who bring with them quite comfortable incomes.

116

There are young professionals settling in rapidly expanding edge cities; they are those who commute to work via computer. There are people with considerable sophistication who could assist towns with declining economic bases determine how to re-create their future.

Amid this great diversity, there is a racism that has characteristics all its own. Competition for limited resources among poor people is a condition that sets the stage and is all too typical in rural communities. Then, when a large producer of livestock establishes a packing plant in a country town and brings in workers from a different ethnic-cultural background and pays them minimum wages, the stage is set for the flare-up of latent racism. Often the workers employed at these plants make so little money that they are eligible for welfare and other services. Their children's need for education and other services that the incoming group brings with it puts pressure on the county or town to provide services which in turn puts pressure on the property tax base to raise people's taxes. Local people who are not doing that well financially themselves resent the people that the company brings in, especially if they wanted the jobs for themselves, and if the imported workers cause taxes to be raised for long-term residents. In essence, the meat packer is asking the county to pay it a subsidy for the opportunity to disadvantage long time residents. The target of long-term residents' resentment is often not the company, which is after all diffuse and hard to locate, but the newcomers.

The poverty and racism of this situation as well as the globalization of agriculture and trade that we have described earlier have taken a disturbing turn in the past five years. During the farm crisis there was an increase in the growth of the radical right and anarchist groups, such as the Posse Comitatis, taking action against representatives of the federal government. That seems to be happening again as the worsening economic situation of some rural counties fans the fires of resentment against the federal government. The rise of "militias" has become especially prominent in the news after the bombing of the federal building in Oklahoma City on April 19, 1995. Waco, Ruby Ridge, and the standoff with the Freemen in Montana are names associated with the rise of hate groups. The widespread sense of powerlessness and loss of control that many rural people feel as well as the genuine injustices that they have undergone have focused rage against a cluster of targets, with the federal government and its agents being the most visible and easily accessible. It would be a mistake for the church to simply decry the violence that these groups practice or occasion without recognizing as well the precipitating injustice that causes these people to cry out.

The co-director of the Town and Country Alliance for Ministry, a congregationally based community organizing group in three rural counties of eastern Iowa, Mary Farwell, suggests the proper stance of the church. She says that what is happening in rural culture is a call for church groups "to confront the system that is denying hope to rural people. There has to be an alternative to extremist groups. We do not offer quick or easy solutions, but we do question a system that does not respond to people or give them hope." Frequently these conflicts seem to arise from an income class base and a sense that the deck is stacked against rural people; often young adult, blue collar, white males feel this way.

The Environment

Inadequate as the attention we can pay it will be, it should be noted that the state of the environment in rural America is a matter of concern. Some 81 percent of the land in the United States is nonmetropolitan; someone is taking care of it, or not. By and large, these people are the ranchers, miners, lumberjacks, fishermen, and farmers who make their living on the land and sea. They have been the representatives of all citizens, and have by and large practiced good stewardship.

There have been numerous conflicts over the way land should be used. There is the conflict between the developers and also those who appreciate and want to hang onto rural aesthetics. There are those who want to preserve the land in a pristine state as over against those who are seen to be exploiting the resources of the land, e.g., in the use of federal lands. There are those who want to use the land for grazing as over against hiking; confinement livestock raising with its attendant manure and odor is producing an enormous backlash by those whom it affects. Then there is the whole issue of the "conventional" use of petrochemicals in farming as over against those who seek to use fewer or little chemicals.

While there are many environmental regulations in place and there is widespread concern about the future of our respiratory and gastronomical intakes (air, water, food), there is some feeling in rural America that farmers and miners and other primary workers are unduly jeopardized by these laws. Specifically, they feel that they are the victims of unfunded initiatives that benefit others without just compensation. In fact, that contributes to the powerlessness that many farmers experience. Similarly, small business owners feel frustrated by environmental laws.

It is, however, the case that substantial gains have been made in the level of acceptance that environmental concerns have realized in the past decade. The rise of sustainable agriculture groups is heartening. We can cite the Practical Farmers of Iowa and the Midwest Organic Growers Association as two examples. Also encouraging is the incorporation of the health of nature as one aspect among many in the Campaign for Sustainable Development and other community development campaigns.

Too often the environment is set over against the economic well-being of rural America. Indeed, we are entering a dangerous time in that environmental gains are under attack from Washington these days, and people may be feeling "compassion fatigue" for the environment. It is encouraging that the churches of the United States have made a concern for the health of creation a matter of priority and that many congregations recognize that this concern is not transient or trivial.[20]

119

The Church and Emerging Trends

How is the church to approach all of these trends? We have tried to describe a number of different rural situations that call for very different ministerial and congregational strategies. There are very real opportunities for faithful Christian witness and mission in every situation. There are some few situations where there is little possible future mission for the church; perhaps these congregations should be incorporated into others; the past of these churches celebrated; and the work of God affirmed in those histories.

This chapter has been addressed primarily to the more difficult case of those churches that are located in counties and towns in decline. There the church is called to the challenging task of encouraging efforts that promise to enhance the quality of life for people there. There are genuine possibilities in almost all cases. To make the most of them will require careful thought, expertise, and community building. That can be done. There are experts in small town development who can enhance value-added agriculture and can assist congregations and communities who want to take on this challenge as Christian outreach and mission to neighbors. Some organizations that may be helpful in this respect are National Catholic Rural Life Conference (Des Moines, IA), Wisconsin Rural Development Center (Mt. Horeb, WI), the Center for Rural Affairs (Walthill, NE), and MSR Center for Rural Ministry (Jefferson City, MO).

**Comments on the Role of Rural Pastors
in Challenging Communities**

Listen to Judy Heffernan, speaking at a Rural Ministry Conference of the Center for Theology and Land, Dubuque, Iowa, on the role of rural pastors in communities that have experienced decline:

"You need to remember how extremely important you are in this context. For many whom you serve, you are what's keeping them going. Not because you have all the answers, not because your faith never falters, not because you've never had any struggles in your own life. You're very important to rural families and to rural communities because you are often seen as the church. I know we lay people are *supposed* to define it differently.

You represent to many the body of Christ present with them in times of trouble. The church is the other major social institution in rural America (along with family). Good stewardship requires that you take good care of yourself as well as of your church.

I do want to suggest two or three things to you: Lead us in powerful worship, powerful and relevant worship. We need to hear it. We need to experience it. Help us, maybe even teach us ways to shore up and deepen our own spirituality. Then, if you would, help us with this vision thing. In this country we have a vision war going on. It is a fight about what will be the compelling vision that guides us. The vision of what kind of community, what kind of society, what kind of family life we want. Then, when I think of clergy I think of few others who know how to do what Truman said of Churchill: namely, mobilize the English language and send it into battle.

You know how to redefine the situation. Help us in our faith communities to hear the power of the Gospel. Help us to see the possibilities in this wilderness in which many folks think we are now existing. Most important of all to you who are clergy, be with us. Help us learn to be for each other what Christ would have us be."

In counties that are growing, congregations are called to a different but also challenging role. They may be called to a ministry of mediating between conflicting groups and building community. They may be called to "signature" or "niche" ministries to a particular group of people moving into their county, or to "county seat" full-service ministries. These are

121

opportunities for church growth and church planting. Just as the church must resist the temptation to be pessimistic about other situations, neither can it equate social and economic prosperity with the kingdom of God. To be sure, there is no virtue in undergoing pain and difficulty but the cultural religion of consumption and success in the United States is a seductive idolatry. The mission of the church is the increase of the knowledge and love of God and the love of neighbor. It is also to call its members to witness to God's justice. In rapidly growing and prosperous rural communities there are plenty of challenges.

To make the picture even more complicated, the church is experiencing emerging trends of its own. One of the most hopeful is the reopening of the question of the optimal shape of congregational leadership. Denominations are learning that the notion of one-priest, one-parish is fading; no longer can denominations afford a standardized model of what pastoral leadership should look like. Sometimes a cooperative parish is more appropriate; sometimes lay leadership is as effective and faithful as ones that are seminary-trained and ordained. The whole question is being revisited in exciting and flexible ways. Our bet is that there will emerge from this transitional period any number of arrangements that fit the particular rural congregation in the particular rural community.

In conclusion, however strenuously we might want to relieve human suffering in rural communities or however much we might want to foster reconciliation and sharing, it will be important for the whole church to remember the source of its hope. It is not we who offer salvation; it is God. Furthermore, the locus of salvation is the whole world; the church is the sign of God's salvation. We continue with a look at the theology of the rural context and then turn to the more practical aspects of how a church can respond to these persistent and emerging trends.

Christian Foundations
and Perspectives

CHAPTER SIX

Re-visioning Rural Ministry: A Theology of Rural Life

Does the church of Jesus Christ have the capacity to respond to what is happening in rural America today? While our answer to that is a clear and resounding yes, Chapter Five has made it evident that the local rural congregation and parish have their work cut out for them.

This book is firmly based on the belief that the church instituted by Jesus Christ, sustained by the Creator of this world, and empowered by the Holy Spirit is committed to following God's guidance for its life in rural America. God is still very much at work in rural communities. Our question, the really difficult question, is this:

How does the church respond to what is happening? What resources does it have to speak to rural peoples in Christ's name?

The first chapter of this book recognized the paradox of rural churches being stalwart centers of hope in the midst of rural decline. They are like finding sunflowers still standing after a hail storm. What accounts for such life and such resilience in these unlikely places? we asked. Why is the church so important in people's lives?

Church members have given us any number of reasons for that: The Christian faith empowers us to understand reality and to face even those aspects that are painful, they say. It offers us rural residents a transformative community of care and work. The church witnesses in worship to the purpose of our lives, to God's sacramental presence with us. The church makes us hunger to share the good news of Christ's salvation with others. The church provides us with moral directions for our lives in a chaotic world.

How Some of These Reasons Get Lived Out

The pastor of a small village church recalls a pastoral visit: "I called upon a man living in our town who was dying of cancer. On the sideboard in the kitchen I noticed a bouquet of fresh wild flowers, and a bowl of fruit. The man smiled and offered me an apple. He told me where the gifts came from. 'Some women from the church came to visit me last night. They brought the flowers and fruit. One of them offered to wash the dishes. At first I thought they were going to try and "save me." I don't have much to do with their church. But they talked with me about cancer and dying. Mostly if people come they talk about the weather, or anything but the fact that I am sick. But these people really wanted to know how I was doing and if I needed anything. They didn't stay long. Before they left they said a prayer with me and they held my hand. No one had ever prayed like that with me before. Will you thank them and ask them to come again?'"

In *Mission: The Small Church Reaches Out* by Tony Pappas and Scott Planting (Judson, 1994), pp. 22–23.

A number of these reasons center around the issue of what we believe as Christians. They have to do with the foundation of what the Christian church believes and what it proclaims, the faith that it is the source of its hope, the God that it worships. Based on Scripture and church tradition this faith in the triune God leads and directs all aspects of our church life—proclamation, service, fellowship, evangelism, worship. What we believe makes a difference. It keeps us going. This understanding of God is what we mean by "theology." It is the focus of Chapter Six, this chapter.

Another group of reasons for the vibrancy of the rural church when it could surrender to despair is that the Christian faith gives us reasons to live, to live even with pain and suffering, to witness to the resurrection of Jesus Christ no matter how bleak the present. Rural people who in the past two decades have experienced a decline in living standards and other losses understand the need for the victory of life over death. We stand on the promise of Christ that he will be with us always.

The church also helps rural residents make sense out of our situation, and gives moral direction to our individual and our corporate lives. Scripture and the church help us understand how we ought to live in light of our beliefs. Certainly the rural church is confronted by no small number of moral issues, as Chapter Five has made abundantly clear. Chapter Seven will build on the beliefs that are laid out here and help us wrestle a bit with the moral issues of soil and community erosion, of how to make a living in a way that celebrates life, and of developing a new ethic for a new day.

Chapters Eight and Nine will get more specific about how the church can go about doing this practically, in its everyday life. That is important. BUT it is also important that the rural church know what it believes as part of its own heritage. What people believe influences how they live. Some would say that what people believe *is* what they live. Theology matters. For too long rural peoples have assumed that theology was not about them, their beliefs, or their lives. It was about books, professional experts, universities, eggheads, or people who sat around doing theology for a living. In some ways they were not too far wrong!

However, theologians have become aware in the past three decades that there is not one single Christian theology. There are **theologies** written by quite particular people, or groups of people. The new insight that has changed theology forever is this: **All theology comes out of a particular community and context.** That context might be the community of Luke-Acts, the community where the author of Luke and Acts lived and worked. It might be the community of European and American university intellectual life. Surely that community, dispersed though it might be, has had a powerful voice in shaping the theology that gets preached from the pulpit and believed in the pew. It might be the African-American community. **OR IT JUST MIGHT BE THE RURAL COMMUNITY.**

We believe that there is a theology born and raised in the rural community and congregation. It has not been written anywhere yet; rather it has been gathered in fragments in various places. Maybe, if Tex Sample is right, the theology of the rural community is an oral, rather than primarily a written, theology.[1] Maybe it is time that we begin to think explicitly about a theology that we believe in our bones and live out of our hearts. There is some value in writing it down. We intend that this book be part of that conversation, a way not just of transmitting the tradition, but also of carrying that tradition on into our time. So, this chapter is an opening wedge, a beginning. We hope that you will be in conversation with it in your churches and communities.

An Indigenous Theology of Context

The first thing that a theology of rural life and ministry wants to know is: **What is God doing here? How is God active in this time and place?** The answer to those questions will begin to direct the church in knowing how to respond to what is happening in rural America. When those questions are asked of rural communities and answered in the light of Christian faith, the results will constitute a theology of rural life and ministry.

This is exactly the way that most exciting theologies are being formulated today. These *are* theologies of context. And that is what we are discovering in this chapter: a theology of

127

the rural context. This theology is not exclusive to rural communities even if it is specific to them; rather, it lifts up particular components of the Christian faith that speak with special force to rural communities. It is a theology of the rural context and church. It is a theology with surprising contours, a theology that points to God's presence. It is a theology of hope, a theology of God's incarnational presence through Christ and the Holy Spirit active in all creation. Rural Christians live in a rare moment of both pain and opportunity; they can make a difference in the future shape of the United States. God is calling clergy and laity to a transforming vision that is unfolding as God guides us into the future. There is not a single blueprint for this future, but our belief that God is present now and into the future makes us confident that we can know the general contours of that unfolding.

It is difficult to speak of "rural America" as though it were all one piece. We know better than that. Nevertheless, it seems to us that there are several themes that predominate in the rural United States. One is clearly the importance of community. Most Americans are looking for community and for God; they are hungry for God if *Newsweek*'s November 28, 1994, cover story, "The Search for the Sacred," captures a contemporary feeling. Even more surprising is a recent Gallup poll finding that 56 percent of Americans have as their number one objective in life "seeking a closer relationship with God."[2] The search for God and the search for a community of fellow believers are joined. It is hard for rural people to imagine that they could be disjointed because the lives of rural peoples are still more integrated with each other than is typical in urban America. Rural people tend to work, play, converse, and worship together. We believe that the integrated community that we experience during the work week helps us see that our faith relates to all other aspects of our lives. The church is the place where all these aspects of our lives come together in God. That is why the church plays such an important role for many rural believers.

128

A New Way of Doing
Theology Locally

Attention to the contextual nature of theology is, by now, widespread. Many observe that theology has always and everywhere been contextual, and that "orthodoxy" or "tradition" is, in fact, nothing other than a series of contextual theologies. Everywhere one looks, the unmistakable flavor of regional and local theological variations is apparent. For Roman Catholics, self-conscious reflection on the role of context in theology dates from the Second Vatican Council's focus on the nature of the church in the modern world. For Protestants, the publication of the World Council of Churches' *Theology in Context, 1972,* brought the term "contextualization" into prominence, defining it as "the capacity to respond meaningfully to the Gospel within the framework of one's own situation."

Local theology is the actual theological production and expression of those who live in a local context. It consists of the tangible and pluriform events of community action and reflection. The medium of expression is rarely writing, because such events are often evanescent. For example, many forms of local theology are oral (narrative, proverb, music, prayer, poetry, etc.). Though pervasively employed, they are spontaneously exercised and fleeting in nature. What is more, they arise from community sources and point toward community ends. Rather than providing a cohesive and coherent system, local theology seeks popular usefulness. It gives people at the grass-roots the theological tools necessary to negotiate the realities and concerns they encounter.

James Nieman, Wartburg Theological Seminary

Church as Community

Theology is not only or even primarily something written in books; it is primarily believed in people's hearts and lived out in their lives. It is a hunger, a longing, a search. It can only continue to be a living faith in a community setting. The church as the Christian community in a particular location is the context in which theology is shaped, believed, lived, and transmitted to others. So it is important to recognize that the church in the rural community is the carrier of beliefs. That is why we focus on the church as a way of framing this chapter.

What people believe is very clear at church get-togethers and it is also present on the sidewalk, the street, the post office, the farm, and the grocery store. We want to affirm that the rural church is the context where rural people work out their beliefs, their theology. That theology has to make sense on the street and in the field.

There are many forces that threaten to unravel the threads of community both in the church and in the rural town. No longer can any rural resident count on community being the natural outgrowth of a homogeneous and traditional culture. There are too many pressures on the local church for that. **This has made the church only more important; it also means that the rural church needs to be more intentional about its role in building community than it once was.**

Community building can take many forms. One key task of the rural church these days is that of calling neighbors to be reconciled with each other and all of us to love justice in our relationships with each other and the society at large. There are so many divisive issues that are impacting rural America that can drive wedges between family members and church members that it is doubly important for the church to recognize that it has the power of reconciliation. It is even more important for the rural church to live out and practice reconciliation. Only if the church is itself a safe community where each person is valued more than anyone's getting ahead, and only if we can work out disagreements openly and justly, can we realize a reconciliation that is deeper than surface politeness. That sort of reconciliation would be evangelistic; that is the sort of community for which we hunger.

There are many forces making for guilt and fear and anger and depression. The church strives *not* to contribute to them. Rather it may be the only institution here or anywhere that is proclaiming the forgiveness of Jesus Christ, that is calling people to salvation and to living lives that embody forgiveness. The ability to live out the grace of God incarnate in Jesus Christ is a dynamic that is vitally needed today. Only on that basis can we have community that is more than superficial friendliness. Thus the task of reconciliation and the task of mediating God's grace are very powerful and very valuable in rural locations. Perhaps this is why the church can be bold in calling friends and neighbors to believe in Jesus Christ, to live out our salvation. This is also why the church is often the place where people can share their pains and struggles and expect others to care about them.

One image of the church that may capture some of this is that the church represents the incarnational presence of Christ.[3] This quality of in-flesh-ment or saturating or embodying is something that is the essence of rural theology. If the church says one thing about God or human beings and lives out another, then it can not be believed. Rural people believe that the church represents God and is supposed to live out Christ's teachings. Obviously the church is not going to do this perfectly; we know that; what this requires is a humility, a confession that we are sinners in need of forgiveness, and a forgiving spirit—forgiving of others and of oneself. In part, this is what it means to witness to the resurrection of Jesus Christ.

The rural church experiences such new life in nature—witness the almost-euphoria of planting in the spring and the celebration of new life and hope budding in that season. Luther said "We witness the resurrection in the unfolding of the leaves each spring." The rural church often embodies being the

131

resurrected presence of Christ in the community—it often is a forgiving and renewing influence in the community. This is what it means for the rural parish to be called to live out that kingdom-life in its own internal life and in the community. That is what we mean when we pray "Thy will be done on earth as it is in heaven."

The Non-Metropolitan Catholic Church: An Overlooked Giant

"A greater *experience of community through friendliness* in the rural and small town people's lifespaces has interesting implications for how they see the parish, its purpose, programming and activities, as well as its public rituals. While the native of a rural locale experiences community in various settings—over coffee, in the post office or at a community meeting—such a person may not be as inclined to look for community in the parish. When a parish and its surrounding community overlap, these community-building functions may be taken care of outside the parish, reserving the church primarily for spiritual activities. The closeness of such communities may account for a greater tendency toward ecumenism and boosterism, except where Catholics constitute a small, class-based minority."[4]

This selection indicates the complexity of the relationship of community and church in rural America. What happens to community when there is an influx of new residents? How does the role of the parish change?

The power that the church has in expressing forgiveness and justice grows out of the way its life is intertwined with that of its members and their location. If anybody has any doubts about just how central the local parish is to its members, just try closing a rural church. Talk about fights! Grandmothers get up and tell how their fathers founded this church 97 years ago and what it has meant to them in the course of their lifetimes. Children of the church come back from the city to testify to its formative power in their lives. Community residents who have only been in the church for funerals, weddings, confirmations, and the annual Christmas pageant write letters to the bishop or executive presbyter. The church is an anchor in the community and in people's lives. It is theirs; why in the world would someone want to take their life-space away from them? Pity the bishop who tries!

The community of church is itself the body of Christ to its rural members. That is to say that rural Christians expect to find community at church in a way that represents Christ's love for them. The church is to be the body of Christ, to be community in a way that transcends the ordinary and rational.

A Theology of Active Presence

There are many other themes that clamor for priority in a rural theology beside community: e.g., land, power, and diversity. One central theological belief, so strong as to qualify as foundational, is that God is actively present in rural life. At their best, rural Christians have had a deep certainty that God is present and active in the world. We think of God as being almost natural, occurring throughout the world and in our lives. The incarnation of Jesus the Christ revealed how much God loved the whole world; in fact God did become present. God continues to be present with us in the Spirit.

Rural people do understand God to be actively present in a way that transcends their own activity. They still believe that there is a moral and spiritual center in the world. Like the Psalmist we ask, "Where can I go from your spirit? Or where can I flee from your presence? If I ascend to heaven, you are there . . . If I take the wings of morning and settle at the farthest limits of the sea, even there your hand shall lead me, and your right hand shall hold me fast" (Ps. 139: 7–10).

Indeed, God is the center who holds despite the winds of change and the chaos of contemporary life. Especially is the church called to imitate and live out that unchanging truth. It is to be the integrating center calling others to abundant life and salvation. We know that Jesus Christ is the Master and Friend who makes sense out of all life and who enables us to live in joy and hope. Christ promised that "if you abide in me, and my words abide in you, ask for whatever you wish, and it will be done for you. My Father is glorified by this, that you bear much fruit and become my disciples. As the Father has loved me, so I have loved you; abide in my love . . . I have said these things to you so that my joy may be in you, and that your joy may be complete" (John 15:7, 8, 9, 11).

What Does the Presence of God Mean for Rural People in Their Everyday Lives?

For rural people this is not a "head" question but a "heart" question. How is God present for them? How does God relate to them? They sing it:

"Trust and obey, for there's no other way, to be happy in Jesus, than to trust and obey"
"What a friend we have in Jesus"
"Amazing grace, how sweet the sound, that saved a wretch like me"

This trilogy of favorite hymns says what God's presence means every day. William B. McClain expresses what gospel songs mean for other, African-American peoples: "The gospel song expresses theology. Not the theology of the university, not formalistic theology or the theology of the seminary, but a *theology of experience*—the theology of a God who sends the sunshine and the rain, the theology of a God who is very much alive and active and who has not forsaken those who are poor and oppressed and unemployed.

> " It is a *theology of imagination*—it grew out of fire shut up in the bones . . . Fear is turned to hope in the sanctuaries and storefronts, and bursts forth in songs of celebration. It is a *theology of grace* that allows the faithful to see the sunshine of His face—even through their tears. Even the words of an ex-slave trader become a song of liberation. It is a *theology of survival* that allows a people to celebrate the ability to continue the journey in spite of the insidious tentacles of racism and oppression and to sing: 'It's another day's journey and I'm glad about it.'"
> *Songs of Zion* (Abingdon, 1981), p. x.
>
> Tex Sample sees McClain's words as expressing the "language of trust and assurance" that "can be found across a range of traditional and oral people and in different traditions and experiences. Many Anglo-European working people in the United States find it expressed in country music. . . . It is hurtin' music, but it also contains hope and a trust and assurance. No matter how bad the loss of lovers, pickups, the farm, the job, the children, country music, at the very least, is hounded with a conviction that life is not supposed to be that way. One does not have to listen long to hear that a brighter day is ahead or that one truly 'did see the light.' "
> *Ministry in an Oral Culture* (Westminster/John Knox, 1994), pp. 81–82.

Rural people know something about economic and social difficulties. They have been living with crisis and decline for fifteen or more years now. That has persuaded many rural people that no matter how hard they work or how much they try, in many ways their lives are out of their control. It has given many rural people a first-hand experience of the grace of God, the real presence of God in their lives. Those hard times have conclusively revealed to many of us that we can not save ourselves, that even our earthly destinies are outside our final control. Farmers know that they can be good money managers;

they can be efficient operators; they can save money by farming with natural inputs; they can do everything right, BUT if they buy at the wrong time, or the rains do not come or come too much, they can still go under. In short, despite our wisdom, our work, and our best efforts, we can still fail. Our best efforts are all-too-human; they are subject to the weather, to economic trends, to policies generated from afar. We have been on the margins and we know that we need salvation beyond ourselves. We can only be saved by God's grace; it is not something we can do. We have to be "washed in the blood of the lamb" because it is finally God who saves us, who counts us as being righteous even though we lost the farm or experienced other trials.

God takes the initiative to save us, not because of anything we did or even failed to do, but only out of God's own love. God in Christ "so loved the world" that God became human and saved us from the power of sin and death. Furthermore, rural peoples know that God is sovereign, that God is powerfully present in the forces of nature and in other people. While Jesus Christ is Redeemer and Friend, there are other blessings that the Creator-God and the Spirit-God have showered on the world. The world was created for the enjoyment of all beings—for delight—for fun—for justice—for community. The world, and here rural peoples include human and animal alike, was designed so that we could all experience the good life, the common good. The sovereign God intended the world to live in total harmony, in *shalom*, so that all life could flourish. God is constantly even yet urging us in that direction; in fact we can see this in the persistence of new life after the winter, in hope in the midst of despair, in resurrection even in the midst of death.

Believing that God is present means that we have a theology of hope and it means that we look for God's presence. We have expectations of God's presence in our rural culture, our towns and countrysides and fields. We **can** celebrate the culture of town and country America because we Christians know that

136

God is present in the best of our customs and values, that God becomes incarnate in Spirit-filled ways. We do not despise our culture but we affirm it. We can also say that God will go into the future with us.

The shape that God's presence takes will vary. Scripture can be seen as a guide to the ways God has been present in the past, most notably in Jesus Christ. What sorts of things did Jesus do? That is what God does. Jesus did many things. He healed those who were broken in body and spirit. He had harsh words for those who mistreated other human beings or who were greedy for too much. Jesus comforted but he also challenged. Jesus clearly stood against those who acted unjustly or who abused the created order. Christian congregations have to wrestle with what specific decisions and actions God is inviting them to undertake.

That journey may start with the recognition that God is calling us to seek first the community of God and God's righteousness, to live as kingdom-people if you will. It is through other people that we can come closer to discerning God's will for our congregation and for rural America. What policies should we advocate and fight for? How should we farm? How can we make this a good place in which to grow up and live? All those questions are ones that we in the Christian community discuss because we know that God is present with us, and that nothing—no government, no money troubles, no divorces, no tragedies, or anything, "will be able to separate us from the love of God in Christ Jesus our Lord" (Rom. 8:38, 39).

A Sense of Place

One distinguishing feature of rural culture is its strong sense of place. Despite the general trend toward homogenization in the U.S.—witness the motel chain that advertises "The best surprise is no surprise" or the popularity of identical fast food restaurants—rural churches and people appreciate the personal and specific; we enjoy the local and the detailed. As one rural proverb has it: "God is in the details." A lot of rural locations bill themselves as "God's country." We like the particular features of our place and we enjoy the particular expressions of faith found in this specific culture.

A Minister from Maine, on the Place of His Call:

"At Starks and West Mills, God's call is all about location, all about place . . . the place where this opportunity came into my life . . . the place where these congregations find themselves poised, and where they perceive God calling them. These are all places in the fullest sense of the word, physical, spiritual, social, and circumstantial: A place for a newly turned 40 year-old seminarian, wet behind the ears on the academic side with a bit more seat of the pants experience.

Starks and West Mills have their needs like most Maine communities, but I can see the richness already in its people and our congregations . . . these few days since Presbytery meeting. Joy and talent in our midst, . . . a place where Evelyn Dow shares the simple joy of seeing Mrs. Doubtfire during 'Joys and Concerns,' . . . where Dolores and Roger's dog Bandit sits in his own seat at the table and has coffee with us during a 'pastoral visit.' I run into Arthur, the organist at West Mills, in the New Sharon farm store.

I can't wait to tell my kids about the handcrafted marionettes he constructs and performs with. Arthur is more than willing to have my daughter Emily accompany him with recorder or violin during worship. She'll like that and I think she'll bless us with her music too.

Which reminds me that both Diane over in West Mills and Chuck in Starks have a wonderful growing connection with kids and what they're doing, not to mention the possibilities across the street from where I sit (Camp at the Eastward).

> It's hard to figure or second guess at this point where God might be stitching this all together, but the connections are hard to ignore."
>
> Jeff Scott, *Chickadee Chatter:* Mission at the Eastward Newsletter, 1995.

The fact that rural people still maintain a distinctive sense of place has great theological potential, which is only now being recognized. It suggests **how we can begin responding to God's presence in rural America,** an issue whose importance we suggested at the beginning of this chapter. A sense of place calls us to attend not to universal places or tendencies, but to the quality of the local place we live. How are healing and justice and worship taking place **here, now?** Beginning with a sense of place is a very rural way of answering that question of how to respond to God's presence.

Surely an appreciation of physical space is an outstanding attribute of rural peoples. We understand that land is life, as one recent Lutheran World Federation report puts it.[5] Millions of people, urban and suburban, are recognizing the centrality of the appreciation for our physical home and its creatures that rural people exemplify. We understand our physical kinship with the world God created. We appreciate the cycle of birth and rebirth that nature expresses through the seasons as a sign of our renewal. Rural people appreciate the fact that land, animals, and our own physical bodies are tied together in an interconnected way. We are in fact part of the environment, our home, God's home, creatures of the Creator and co-creators at the same time.

It is not just any land or any physical space that is appreciated; it is the particularity of **this** rural land and **this** space. That makes it precious to us, if not sacred. Indeed, we rural people can become almost idolatrous about this being our land, our place; we can assume that the land is ours to take care of as we choose. On the whole, however, an appreciation of local land translates into a recognition that this place is God's garden, a

139

biblical metaphor with existential roots in rural places. That makes agriculture a vocation and food at least potentially sacramental. One strong theme in the Roman Catholic tradition sees the world as sacramental, as embodying the grace of God. This theme is similar to one in the Reformed tradition, which views the beauty of the earth as revelatory of God's own beauty.

The sense of place also includes the feeling that we share this place with others, particular others who are our neighbors.[6] There is a community understanding of the Creator image of God that rural Christians appreciate. They like the egalitarian and democratic features of that aspect of God. As Walter Brueggemann writes:

> Creation not only works for the powerful, the mighty, and the knowledgeable. It works as well for the faint, the powerless, the hopeless, and the worthless. It works by giving seed to the sower and bread to the eater (Isa. 55:10). It works so that strength is renewed. It is the creation that precludes weariness and faintness, and invites walking, running, and flying.[7]

If the land is a garden, then we rural folks are the gardeners. There is a corporate dimension to the care for the land. The sense of place is, at its best, not individualistic; it does not separate human beings from each other; rather it connects them to the land **and to each other**. This is our place; we are its gardeners.

One of the great strengths of life in the country is that rural peoples still maintain the ideal of having their lives intertwined with those who are their neighbors. They still believe that people should be able to count on those who share their place. The ideal of community and shared place are very much alive in the rural United States.

It is important, nay vital, that Christian congregations have some sense of what it means to be community, to both support others and to depend upon them. For one of us the premier example of this was the fact that the people of Zachary,

Louisiana, authorized their doctor to go to New Orleans and find them a dentist in 1939. The dentist Dr. Lane found was his father. *Congregations* would do well to understand that God so interlinked God's life with humankind and that of other species that we are called to demonstrate a holistic care for the other. We are to live in such a way that others can trust us. We meet Christ in the neighbor.

The quality of relationship that is indicated by our striving for community has much to do with what we call salvation. It indicates a desire for completion, a hunger to overcome alienation and estrangement—from God and neighbor and world. Precisely this lack of intimacy afflicts us; Allen Bloom writes that "isolation, a lack of profound contact with other human beings, seems to be the disease of our time."[8] We in the U.S. appear to be losing our capacity for love and friendship; many report feeling a profound loneliness in their lives. Not only is there a hunger for personal intimacy with others, there is also a hunger for public belonging, for community. There is a political aspect to our salvation; we wish to be a part of a larger purposeful community. While intimacy and community may not be the whole of salvation, it seems safe to say that they will at least accompany whatever else salvation is.

Christ calls us to public relationships as well as to personal ones. This becomes quite evident with a rural sense of place. If our rural towns and countryside are gardens, then we Christians are called to be gardeners. We are to care for the quality of this place we call ours and recognize to be God's home as well. Our moral responsibility, part of our sanctification, becomes caring for the place where we live. This is part of Luther's belief that we are to be little Christs to each other. Thus the political task for Christians is their corporate responsibility for the quality of life in their community. The moral question becomes, "What is the quality of life in my community? What does justice commend here?"

Rural theology commends a justice of the local here and now rather than a justice appropriate to there and then; there

141

is an expectation that spiritual meaning can be found in the routine everyday of individual and social life and hopefully shared in a congregation as well as shaped by a congregation.

The Hazards of Globalism

Doug Walrath, in a little pamphlet entitled "The Hazards of Globalism," warns us that a love affair with global issues (exemplified by communications local churches sometimes receive from denominational headquarters) may lead to the conclusion that "vital ministry is most likely to be carried on by someone else, some place else." Walrath is saying that the reaction against localism has gone entirely too far in the opposite direction. Furthermore, Christians are now tempted to do mission vicariously; to believe that the most important reaching out we do is to send money. However, we are called not just to support mission, but to do mission, to be ministers and missionaries. We need to get our hands dirty in the service of the church to others.[9]

A theology of God's presence and sense of place calls us to act on our beliefs, to practice our faith. Rural Christians understand justice in local terms and begin to act on that belief close to home. It is no surprise when that local beginning translates into global action.

Respecting Otherness

Sometimes a contextual theology is built on qualities that are present in the location. However, sometimes it is the case that a theology of context must call for a transformation of qualities that have detracted from the spiritual quality of a place. It would be remiss of us not to say that the latter is the case with this emphasis on respecting otherness. We rural people have sometimes failed to recognize that the Holy Spirit may be calling us to a different future through the gifts of otherness. Changes and different groups of people may be God's gifts to us.

In some ways it is easy to understand the reasons for resistance to change and closedness to other ethnic and national groups. Rural peoples have witnessed many changes, almost all of them for the worse. It is hard to welcome changes that are associated with socioeconomic decline. Furthermore, a number of meat-packing and food-producing rural industries have imported laborers of different racial, ethnic, and national origins into predominantly white, Christian, rural populations of European ancestry. Those industries have paid minimum wages, which has put pressure on already strained rural social services departments (welfare, schools, police). That has increased pressure to raise taxes. (Do you know that **twelve** languages are spoken by students in the public schools of Spencer, Iowa?) Workers were imported for those jobs at a time when longtime inhabitants were struggling. Instead of providing economic development and relief for local people, this business decision added to their economic burden. It also fanned rural resentment to those imported. To blame those imported is to misplace our anger, and may lead to our neglecting the action needed to confront the real culprits and call for remedial steps.

However understandable, such resistance to otherness blocks the Spirit's leading us into the future, a future of new creation. Hospitality to strangers is as central in the Bible as any injunction except that of worshiping and glorifying God. We are to be hospitable because we may be doing unto the least of these as unto our Lord (Matt. 25:31–46); we are to welcome strangers because we were strangers and slaves in Egypt (Lev. 19:34). God is particularly present in the stranger, the guest, the other. Thus the foundation of rural theology—God's active presence—is reinforced in respecting otherness.

Why Respect Otherness?

Our places can be impoverished or enriched by our capacity to respect otherness. Much can be lost if we fail to respect the gifts of other people, however different they are. Much can be gained by appreciating their gifts.

So Tony Pappas tells the story of Clayton, a seventy-year old who is legally still a minor. "Clayton pumped gas there on Block Island until his retirement. He sometimes had trouble making change for people, and some of the rich yacht owners would get impatient with his slowness.

Clayton never missed church except during the tourist season. He was usually at church an hour and a half early folding bulletins, greeting worshipers as they came in the door, and making sure everyone felt welcome and comfortable. When he had to be absent from church, before his retirement, he always filled his offering envelope every week and brought all of them wrapped in a rubber band when he returned in October.

When Clayton hung up his gas hose for the last time, church members tricked him into a retirement dinner at the church. He sat at the head table for the first time in his life. Fellowship Hall was packed. Fifty or sixty people turned up to honor old Clayton. We all loved him. Clayton certainly was different. He was other. In a way, of course, we all are."

Being "good neighbors" to each other grows out of a sense of place. What holds people together as citizens is that they live in the same place. When each person has a stake in the rural locale they inhabit, they have more reason to collaborate. Face-to-face collaboration can produce neighborliness—even among people who don't like each other, even among people who are different from each other, or who threaten each other. Deep in the rural psyche runs the Christian norm of neighborliness. A strong sense of place helps us include others in our circle of neighbors.[10]

The place to begin respecting otherness is to recognize that rural America itself is not homogeneous. It is likely to become even less homogeneous. While the myth of rural homogeneity dies hard, die it must. There is not one standard, one way of thinking, one way of doing things, one class, one race, or one denomination. The way to respect otherness is to affirm differences, learn from those that are healthful, cooperate with and through them, understand them and, indeed, contribute our own otherness to them.

Otherness is a gift to be appreciated and entered into dialogue with because God might be speaking through it. The hope for our future in rural America is to recognize that we have gifts which, in concert with those of others, offer new hope for the future.

Through Brokenness to Hope

Quite some time back, one of the leaders of the Town and Country Church Movement noted that American Christianity had never had to deal with socioeconomic decline or failure. E.W. Mueller also suggested that rural churches might be the source of a theology that could deal with such downward mobility. It may still be the case that a rural theology could lead the way in this regard. Rural peoples may be the first to face the fact that they cannot by themselves create a meaningful future. They receive that future as a gift from God; they stand in the power of the Spirit and receive their lives only after having lost them. By reframing the future as one in which God's promises and trustworthiness can be counted on, we will be freed to welcome others, to see changes as opportunities for re-creating communities of neighborliness and good will.

Contained within the statistics on rural poverty and family abuse, eroding health care and economic stagnation are the pain and suffering many people have experienced. It is vital that the rural church address that pain and suffering not by denying it, but by discerning how God might be present there.

Basically we want to affirm those theologies which assert that God is present with and suffers with those who are in great pain. God does not deny pain and suffering nor make it go away. God does stand with those who suffer; indeed, the death of Jesus Christ is the prime example of the God who suffers and knows the suffering of people and of nature. Dorothee Soelle suggests that

> All suffering persons are in the presence of God. There is no "if." God does not forget. The *praesenti dei* is never merely an observing presence but always in pain or joy. Without God's pain, God is not really present but only turns up like the president of a government occasionally visiting the people. But God does participate in our suffering. God is here and suffers with us.[11]

An experience that speaks forcefully to this topic is Jean Vanier's work in L'Arche communities for the mentally disabled. In a little book, *From Brokenness to Community*, Vanier affirms that suffering and brokenness may be the path to community and salvation. "People may come to our communities because they want to serve the poor; they will only stay once they have discovered that they themselves are the poor," he writes. His suggestion is that we are all the poor in some way; even the most affluent do not escape pain and suffering. But "Jesus came to bring the good news to *the poor*, not to those who serve the poor . . . We are called to discover that God can bring peace, compassion, and love through *our* wounds."[12] The way this may happen is that

> The cry for communion in the poor and broken makes us touch our own inner pain. We discover our own brokenness and the barriers inside of us, which have gradually been formed during our childhood to save us from inner pain. These barriers prevent us from being present to others, in communion with others; they incite us to compete and to dominate others. It is when we have realized this that we cry

out to God. And then we meet the "Paraclete," the Holy Spirit; literally, "the one who answers the cry" . . . It is not possible to receive the Spirit unless we cry out, and unless that cry surges up from the consciousness of our own wound, our pain, and our brokenness.[13]

Only with the recognition and confession of our own suffering and pain can genuine community with others and dependence on God be born.

This may seem a merely negative statement in the ethos of the U.S. these days. We believe that hiding our brokenness seems essential and negative **only** to those who think they have no alternative. That brokenness, if it goes unconfessed, becomes a nemesis that may take several forms. One of those is to depress our thinking and render us powerless. It can also immobilize us if we do not confess and deal with it. Such confession is the basis of community and corporate action. Paradoxically enough, the recognition and confession of brokenness is based on Christian hope, it strengthens that hope, and generates community.

"THIS IS YOUR LAND" (tune: Finlandia)

This is Your land, O God of all creation,
　　The land by which You give us daily bread.
This is Your land, and all eyes look to You, Lord,
　　From Your good earth by grace we all are fed.
This is Your land. You let us make our homes here,
　　And we enjoy the blessings 'round us spread.
This is our land, but only as a trust, Lord.
　　We are Your stewards, here to do Your will.
This is our land, but not as our possession;
　　Though we may tend it, it is Your land still.
This is our land, our place of earthly labor,
　　Our land to love, conserve, preserve and till.

You give us life on farms, in towns and cities:
    All bound together, one community.
But sin and pride and greed for wealth and power
    Threaten that life, destroy our unity.
Our rural life is sacrificed to idols:
    To dogs of war and of "prosperity."
Let righteousness roll down like living waters,
    And justice like an everflowing stream.
Let us be neighbors, caring for each other,
    Working together to preserve the dream:
A life on farms, in rural towns and cities,
    God's land and ours, community redeemed..

This hymn was written by Rev. Edward Kail, then the pastor of the Mt. Ayr Parish, United Methodist Church, Mt. Ayr, Iowa. One evening in 1985, with the farm crisis that was then consuming the Midwest heavy on his heart, Ed took out his guitar and wrote this hymn. Ed is now the occupant of the Endowed Chair in Town and Country Ministry at Saint Paul School of Theology in Kansas City, Missouri.

The rural church itself can recognize its own brokenness; it can remember that it is God's instrument, that it does not stand in its own strength. Thus it will be empowered to confess its shortcomings and gather power from its faith heritage and trust in God's future. God calls the church to faithful and effective witness. The rural church is called to make disciples. Its concepts of mission and evangelism are to be both true and transformative. Christians should not glory in suffering or defeat, but they **can** deal with those demons and go on to live lives of joyful mission. They can share good news and work for God's kingdom of justice and peace.

Sometimes pain and suffering are due to forces over which we have no effective influence. God stands with us in our suffering; we are called to stand in solidarity with others in their suffering. Being in genuine solidarity is to be in compassion, to be present with the other in whom God is also present, to suffer together.

Reclaiming Our Power

However, when the source of suffering and pain can be changed, when it is the outgrowth of injustice, then we as Christians cannot ignore the injustice that could be transformed. Individual Christians and the church are called to stand with those whose suffering cannot be relieved: to render palliative aid (food, shelter, clothing, financial assistance, helping people become self-reliant again) when that is needed, and to work at changing structures of injustice when we can. We are called to act in transformative ways.

Rural people have an ambivalent relationship with power and powerfulness. On the one hand, there is the tradition of rugged individualism, which affirms that "I can do it myself." This is a boasting of one's own power. On the other hand, there is the sense of a total lack of power, of being under the control of external forces and unable to extricate oneself. This sense of powerlessness has grown stronger in the countryside.

Theologically, the issue of power has been regarded ambivalently by the church. Power has too often been seen as prelude to corruption. These negative connotations of power emerge from an understanding of power as the ability to carry out one's project regardless of others' wishes. That sort of ruthless disregard for others is at variance with Christ's example, surely. However, if power is understood simply as the ability to act, positively and negatively, in the service of good or evil, then power can be seen as positive. It is our intention to refurbish the notion of power in and for the sake of the rural congregation.

Rural people's sense of powerlessness is not all in their minds; they **have** lost economic and political power to the rest of the country. U.S. culture has tended to concentrate power in urban areas, although many people in cities are also less well off than they used to be. There has been a "delocalizing" effect of this trend which accompanies centralization.

The church sometimes feeds into a sense of powerlessness. It sometimes supports a theology which depreciates power or sees power as only negative. Rural congregations cannot afford such counsel. There are always power relations at work; power is a dimension of any relationship. To pretend otherwise is itself a dynamic with power implications.

What Is the Nature of This Power?

The church has long affirmed that we Christians partici-pate in the power of Jesus Christ through the work of the Holy Spirit. Too often the church has pretended that this power was only the power of individual piety and that its members had no earthly power. That is just flat wrong and in fact it disguises from us the real issue, which is how Christians use their power. Dorothee Soelle spells out the power of Jesus Christ that is available to every Christian:

"Christ is a name which for me expresses solidarity, hence suffering with, struggling with. Christ is the mysteri-ous power which was in Jesus and which continues on and sometimes makes us into 'fools in Christ,' who, without hope of success and without an objective, share life with others. Share bread, shelter, anxiety, and joy. Jesus' attitude toward life was that it cannot be possessed, hoarded, safeguarded. What we can do with life is to share it, pass it along, get it as a gift and give it on."

Theology for Skeptics: Reflections on God, p. 93.

Beyond this there are many who do have quite a bit, both financially and in terms of their abilities, to pass on in Christ's power and service.

The corrective to the sin of ignoring our power is to move into the future confident that the God of the past will move into that future before us and with us guiding us. The doctrine of the Holy Spirit emphasizes God's power at work in our lives. What that involves is a realistic estimate of what *we can do*, given **God's** wisdom and strength. Rural peoples need to recognize our power, our ability to act. If we were to realize our corporate power, we could be effective in representing our concerns politically and ecclesially.

Christians believe that their gifts and abilities are God-given; they are not simply skills that individuals develop on their own. These instruments of power should be devoted to the service of the neighbor, as Calvin said. We are called to our vocations to exercise power; we are to be the agents of Christ. The parable of the talents (Matt. 25:14-30) certainly counsels us against both slothfulness and underestimating our gifts. Our daily work—our vocation—is one place our power can be realized in God's service.

Furthermore, if the world is the arena of God's active presence, we are summoned out of passivity. We are to support God's purposes; we are to use our power in ways that express God's purposes *which we know in general*. We can use our abilities to discern how those purposes can be actualized *in our specific situations*.

Finally, our powers are sustained by the community of Christians and others. We are interconnected with them. Our interaction and active cooperation with them build both of us up. We can approach the future with hope because God is there. We know that God acts through others, family and friends who challenge and support us.

Sometimes the exercise of power will get caught up in struggle and in conflict; that is almost inevitable. However, even there, maybe especially there, God is present. Struggle can be good. The rural church can call us out of politeness and civility. The church must realize its promise as a community of intimacy, worship, and just action. The principalities and powers of this world no longer assume that church people will be active in advocating for God's purposes; they are wrong!

Finding out how our powers feed into God's purposes is extremely liberating. We rural peoples need not accept what distant others offer us by way of policy or governance. Being aware that we stand in God's power, we can decide on that basis who and what we will support. It may also mean that we can take action as a corporate body that will result in more just and more spiritually enriching life in rural communities.

We have, throughout this theology of rural life, alluded to the church because it is the body of first loyalty for the followers of Jesus Christ. It is the constituency for whom theology is written and which does theology in its life. Thus it is important for each parish, each community of faith, to wrestle with the theology appropriate to its place, its life. What sort of congregational life and mission could witness to God's power as expressed in this outpost of God's community?

CHAPTER SEVEN

Moral Principles and Issues in Rural Life

The crisis the church confronts in rural communities serves as a wake-up call to respond to the new reality of social and environmental erosion. When we take time to do serious reflection about what is unfolding around us, what has happened in the twentieth century with regard to human relationships with the earth and with each other is a deep-seated contradiction to the biblical principles of caregiving and renewal. At present, we do not have a just society. In fact, we tolerate injustice. However, we are now responding, worldwide, to a wake-up call that is manifested in recent years by the growing recognition of environmental and social discontinuities. The encouraging trend in our contemporary world is that we are beginning to recognize the need and the challenge to move ourselves onto a more sustainable path.[1]

As suggested in the opening chapter of this book, the churches located in rural America have an awesome responsibility to provide a clear voice of judgment, vision, and hope in order to enable not simply the local town or village, but also the whole national community, to move onto a sustainable path in agriculture, forestry, and fisheries.

Why Care and Work for Renewal?

Before considering the fundamental social and ecological issues needing to be addressed by the churches, it is important to ask the question, "Why care about these matters in the first place?" Why care about the land and the people who are geographically so closely related to the land? Why care about the prospects for future generations? Why care about the welfare and future of non-human life? At the outset of examining moral principles and issues involved in rural America, it is important to shed light upon our motivation about caring for the community of life and working for its renewal and sustenance for many generations to come.

Why care about the future? One can conclude that caring about any person or thing, non-human life, soil, water, air, climate stability, the prospects for food for tomorrow, the shape and future of our fields of endeavor is our only way of expressing gratitude to God for life and our opportunity to participate in it. Finding a way to say "thanks" is what makes us human. Choosing to care is an act of responsible freedom. The freedom to choose to be responsible, or to care about the future, ought to be understood as a basic human right. If, for whatever reason, we are unable to choose freely to care, we are denied a fundamental element of our humanity. Why do we work so hard in our endeavors to assure the welfare of future generations whom we will never know? Why work hard to design, for example, an agriculture that meets the needs of the present without compromising the ability of future generations to meet their needs for food and fiber? One can conclude that we ought to care because we have a basic human need to say "thanks" for the wondrous miracle of life. The motivation of gratitude is high on the scale of moral maturation and is the essence of ethical decision making. This way of thinking leads us beyond simplistic ethical foundations of rewards and punishments or enlightened self-interest. Caring and working for the renewal of the health and integrity of the land and all its creatures in ways that perpetuate life in its full beauty and integrity are our only real ways to say "thanks."

The Principle of Caring Our faith tradition calls us to a joyful responsibility to be caregivers and to serve the renewal of every aspect of God's creation. In the New Testament we learn about praying for the coming of God's kingdom on earth, just as it is in heaven (Matt. 6:10–11). Our self-understanding as a people of biblical faith is that we are called and sent into the world to be instruments of God's renewal. Likewise, we understand ourselves to be instruments of God's justice. And, in Christ, we are transformed people called to witness to what is good and right and perfect (Rom.12:1–2).

In the Bible we see that humanity is challenged to organize its communities in ways that will result in caring for the whole earth and providing justice for all its inhabitants. This is a very profound ecological thought. Caregiving is a demanding moral principle. In the Bible, and as also seen in biological and physical sciences, all species of life are parts of the whole community of life (Hos. 4:1–3). The human species has great responsibility for the maintenance of justice and integrity for all life including all of its own members. Thus, we have the responsibility to see that human relationships with each other and the earth itself are always enhancing, regenerative, and therefore just. Consequently, sound biblical perspectives about creation and justice cause us to raise questions about whether or not our contemporary scientific, technological, and industrial organizations, particularly in agriculture, forestry, and fishing, contribute to the health of croplands, forests, grasslands, watersheds, aquifers, and human and non-human communities of life. If not, then we are concerned to find ways that will.

Do our modern ways help to guarantee the health and welfare of all life forms and their patterns of sustenance both for now and for the many generations that are yet to follow us? These are difficult questions that need to be asked if the society is to regain its understanding of the full meaning of justice and

155

righteousness. Our present way of measuring profit or loss does not account for diminished or lost resources nor the impact of production processes upon the assurance of the health of soil, water, and air resources. Classical economics fail to account properly for many of the social, natural resource use and environmental costs associated with production and consumption. What we measure as growth may in fact be an illusion when we fail to account for the reduction of natural capital. We must ask, "What is left for future generations?" We need more adequate accounting systems.[2]

The Principles of Renewal and Sustainability The moral principle of caregiving points to another principle, or moral guideline designed to steer us in the direction of caregiving. This is the principle of renewal. In Christ, all things are made new. Today, the entire world is responding to the renewing vision, challenge, guideline, and goal of "sustainable development" that is defined as "development that meets the needs of the present without compromising the ability of future generations to meet their own needs."[3]

Eco-justice Issues: Global and Local Perspectives

Our evaluation about what is happening in rural communities or the rural reality today needs to be focused on God's mandate to care for creation and to provide for justice in all our relationships with each other and the earth itself. This involves present as well as future generations. It is difficult to comprehend the enormity of loss of the nation's soil and water resources, its grasslands and forests, and stress and extinction of its animal and plant species. All of these resources are being utilized far beyond their regenerative capacities. Soil loss continues to equal, or even exceed, the losses suffered during the "dirty thirties." In general, the nation's rangelands, like the world-wide pattern of degradation, are overgrazed. Forest harvests exceed replanting. Animal, plant, and insect species are in rapid decline.[4]

If justice is to prevail, it will be based upon the principle of sustainability; a principle that is as real and unyielding as those, for example, of aerodynamics or thermodynamics. A society can violate the principle of sustainability in the short term, but not in the long run. As Lester Brown has observed:

> Over the long term, species extinction cannot exceed species evolution; soil erosion cannot exceed soil formation; forest destruction cannot exceed forest regeneration; carbon emissions cannot exceed carbon fixation; fish catches cannot exceed the regenerative capacity of fisheries; and human births cannot exceed human death.[5]

One of the major health concerns of the nation is pollution and toxicity in the food system. Most of our surface water resources and a good deal of our nation's aquifers are laden with petro-chemical run-off from farming enterprises. Some of these chemicals then appear in plant and animal tissue that we eventually ingest in the food we eat.

The decline of rural populations and the farmer's share in the marketplace continues to be unjust. For example, although costs of production have escalated since the beginning of this century, market prices for the major grain commodities remain roughly the same today as then. In constant dollars adjusted for inflation during the period of 1910 to 1990, American agribusiness grew from a 75 billion dollar enterprise in 1910 to a 300 billion dollar activity by 1990. During this same period, the value of agricultural inputs (tractors, machinery, tools, fuel, feed, seed and farm chemicals) grew from 11 to 75 billion dollars. The economic return in gross sales to farmers was 30 billion dollars in 1910. It peaked at 55 billion dollars at the end of the Second World War in 1945, and has steadily declined since then to about 30 billion dollars in 1990. Thus, gross income to the farming sector represents about 10 percent of today's American agribusiness enterprise.[6] What has happened and what continues to unfold with reference to these issues is a profound contradiction to normative biblical wisdom about caregiving, renewing, and justice. The warning found in Isaiah 5:8 about joining field to field until nowhere can the people be found and the social consequences that ultimately follow is as relevant today as it was in the seventh century B.C.E. The task that challenges the churches is to revitalize struggling rural communities and to forge new working relationships for a more secure economic future. David Ostendorf, the first director of PrairieFire, states the challenge in the following way:

> What is needed is a transforming encounter with the prevailing economic and political powers that daily grind down people and the communities. The unraveling of the social fabric will stop only when the people decide that their collective loss of control over economic and political decision-making has gone far enough and that democratic ideals are no longer for sale.[7]

One of the best descriptions of the crisis that we face today challenged the world community more than twenty years ago. Barbara Ward and Rene Dubos wrote in the preparatory material for the United Nations Conference on the Human Environment:

> In short, the two worlds of man [sic]—the biosphere of his inheritance, the technosphere of his [sic] creation—are out of balance, indeed potentially in deep conflict. And man [sic] is in the middle. This is the hinge of history at which we stand, the door of the future opening on to a crisis more sudden, more global, more inescapable, and more bewildering than any ever encountered by the human species and one which will take decisive shape within the life span of children who are already born.[8]

Indeed, we are caught in the midst of this conflict and have little time left to provide for its resolution. The United Nations Conference on Environment and Development (UNCED), meeting at Rio de Janeiro in 1992, with its challenge to move onto a path of sustainable development is a hopeful sign that we can respond positively to new challenges. The world community has now recognized, at least in a general way, that the direction in which humanity is traveling is not sustainable. There is the added recognition that in view of the moral concept of safeguarding the welfare of future generations, our way does not provide for justice, in that we are using nature's capital, leaving little inheritance for future generations.

From the 1970s to the mid-1990s, the nations of the world have held, under the organizing auspices of the United Nations, major conferences to assess trends in population growth, food and the extent of cropland loss, desertification, the status of women, laws for the management of the resources of the seas, the impact of armaments upon social and economic development, fresh water resource conservation, climate stability and global warming. Strategies for reversing the negative trends in these areas of concern have been identified and, in significant instances, acted upon.[9] However, what is being undertaken is far less than what is needed for assuring planetary survival. Thomas Berry in his book, *The Dream of the Earth*, describes the contemporary challenge with these words:

> The issue now is of a much greater order of magnitude, for we have changed in a deleterious manner not simply the structure and functioning of human society: we have changed the very chemistry of the planet, we have altered the biosystems, we have changed the topography and even the geological structure of the planet, structures and functions that have taken hundreds of millions and even billions of years to bring into existence. Such an order of change in its nature and in its order of magnitude has never before entered either into earth history or into human consciousness.[10]

We are in the center of the conflict of the biosphere of our inheritance and the technosphere of our inheritance. Never before has humanity faced such bewildering challenges. These threats to planetary health and stability were not in our imaginations even forty years ago. In spite of clairvoyant authors such as Barbara Ward, Rene Dubos, and Lester Brown and also many local, national, and international study groups and conferences, we often wonder why these concerns have yet to be adequately acted upon. The reasons that have led to society's reluctance to wrestle with these matters are many. In our nation, individual rights continue to prevail over matters of community welfare. Corruption and greed, manifested in a vast array of vested interests, continue to shape the way the society faces historically unprecedented issues. We continue to tolerate injustice. Our system of accounting deceives us because it does not count the costs of pollution nor the loss of resources in the process of production. The society remains largely unaware of the fragile structure of natural systems upon which the whole community of life depends. We ignore addressing the urgent needs of our times, including planetary health and threats to planetary survival, because we feel paralyzed by complexities. We are all preoccupied with short-term rather than long-range outcomes. We remain ferociously defensive of the status quo. We are confused about inconclusive evidence and contradictory findings about climate stability, deforestation, carbon emissions, and chlorofluorocarbon impact on the ozone shield. Our media is hesitant to report these critical issues adequately. Theologically, we cling to a dualistic tradition that for nearly 2000 years has separated us philosophically from the earth. We find that numbness about these matters leaves us unable to feel pain and to face the facts of life in our time. Our tendency to self-deception leads us to deny reality.[11]

Central to the resolution of the issues we are called to address is the rural response. Unless the health of croplands and rangelands is preserved, there is no way that humanity will much longer be able to feed itself.[12] Rural ministry has everything to do with the outcome of the race to balance food supplies with predictable population numbers, patterns of resource consumption, pollution, and the carrying capacity of the ecosystems in which we find ourselves. In part, achieving equilibrium will be the result of assuring justice for the poor and the elevation of the status of women of the world.

160

To illustrate how these global issues could impact the rural sector of American communities within less than a half-century, one needs to look no farther than the predictable impact China will make throughout the world and certainly upon the United States. By the year 2030, China's population is predicted to increase by another five hundred million people. As China continues to expand its economy and its people are consequently able to improve their diet, greater demands will be placed on the production of livestock as well as food and feed grains. As this occurs, China, most of whose landscape is semi-arid rangeland and desert, continues annually to lose about 1 percent of its agricultural lands to urban and industrial sprawl and the erosion of soil resources. By 2030, China's estimated need for importing additional food and feed grains is calculated at between 200 and 300 million tons. Currently, total world grain exports are at the 200 million ton level; this amount is being purchased by nearly 100 nations. It takes little imagination to estimate the impact of all these phenomena upon the grain-producing regions of the North American continent. The pressures that will fall upon the U.S. agricultural economy and upon the land itself are almost beyond prediction, for as Lester Brown forecasts, "when China turns to world markets on an ongoing basis, its food scarcity will become the world's scarcity; its shortages of cropland and water will become the world's shortages." He goes on to say that "the shock waves from this collision (between expanding human demand for food and the limits of some of the earth's most basic natural systems) will reverberate throughout the world economy with consequences that we can now only begin to foresee."[13]

Unless American agriculture is organized within the next two decades to insure that production does not exceed the regenerative caring capacity of the grain-growing regions, maximizing production at any cost will likely occur. If safeguards are not in place, soils could be lost at greater rates than are presently measured. Highly erodible lands, presently held in reserve, might be opened once again to annual cropping and to the constant and unpredictable threats of drought and wind. As was the case in the early 1970s, land prices might escalate, setting the stage for another round of economic instability for the rural communities situated within the grain belt of the Plains states. New fortunes might be made in the short term, but because of increased stress placed upon fragile prairie ecosystems, the resource base could be further eroded leaving the health and welfare of future generations in question.

The churches in the rural sector serve within this new and historically unprecedented context of global proportions. As described in Chapter Two, rural church history provides few precedents to equip itself for ministry today and tomorrow. The need to revision rural ministry is clear. Above all else in our moment of history is the need for a significant prophetic voice of judgment and hope.[14] The churches need to regain their commitment to the biblical mandate for the caring and renewal of the land. With a renewed reading of the Scriptures, they can foresee the consequences that beset society if the society fails in its responsibility to care for the land in sustaining ways, generation after generation. Rural ministry must be re-visioned if it is to provide a prophetic voice and a redemptive witness.

New Tasks for a New Era

When the immigrant communities settled across the North American continent, pastors and priests soon followed in response to the expressed needs of these new communities for leadership in the establishment and maintenance of the church on the frontier. The mission of the church was organized to reach these isolated people. Consequently, within less than a century, churches appeared at almost every crossroad. The congregations were served. Land and forest resources were assumed to be without limits. The frontier abounded with wildlife. Many of the continent's underground water resources were unknown. Chemical fertilizers and pesticides were yet to be invented. Rural communities were isolated from the rest of the world. But today, all of this has changed. The primary question is not simply the survival and well-being of frontier communities and congregations. Rather, it is the survival of the planet as we presently know it.

In the past two decades many of these issues were separated from the primary mission of the church. They were dealt with as "specialized ministries" or "social issues" or even "social ministry." We failed to recognize how these environmental, economic, racial, and other issues impacted the congregation. Now we do. The rural church understands now that these issues are up close and personal; they affect the lives of those in our pews and in our communities.

Now, the ministry of the churches includes witness and service for the renewal of the ecological health of the land and its people. This is new! Consequently, the vision of rural ministry expands. The new tasks that now challenge the churches involve earth caring and service for the renewal, and even enhancement, of the land. Today, the churches are being called to minister to the needs of the whole world for the sake of the world. We must think globally and act locally on behalf of the health and welfare of the whole.

Members of congregations may be engaged with many institutions working for renewal through sustainable development. They are motivated by the words of scripture that have been identified throughout the chapters of this book. The challenge placed before the church is to meet needs that are not now being addressed by others. The need is to fulfill a role that is complementary to what secular organizations are doing. This is to say, the churches are being called to those tasks that support and sustain all people of good will who work for sustainable and therefore more just futures. Our next section will begin to answer the question of how congregations can address these tasks.

Congregational Life and Mission

CHAPTER EIGHT

Visioning Rural Ministry Again for the First Time

The church has a vision, a covenant with God that really began in Genesis when God saw everything that God had made, and indeed it was very good. God created us in the divine image, created us into community that we should live together, care for each other, have relationship with each other and with God.

God has called us into relationship. Because we are created in the image of God, that gives each person an equal and sacred value—Roman Catholic social teaching names this the "dignity of the human person." Christian and Jewish traditions offer us the vision of *shalom* which requires us to re-establish "right relationships" with each other and with God. *Shalom* is a call to justice in the whole community and for the entire habitat. *Shalom* is an inclusive notion of justice that extends even to the rest of God's creatures and the whole of creation. Restoring right relationships takes us farther than respecting individual rights. It pushes us to begin to see ourselves as part of a community, even as members of an extended but deeply inter-connected global family, and ultimately as strands in the web of life that we—all of God's creation—share and depend upon.[1]

A Re-vision for Rural America

In our discussions about this book, we have moved toward a new vision for rural America. While some differences remain among us, these are central tenets of that vision:

1. Agriculture and other natural resource-based economic activity should be sustainable and renewable.

2. Rural persons/families should be able to enjoy the just fruits of their labor.

3. Rural people should be presented the good news of the gospel and encouraged to respond by ever praising Jesus Christ as their Savior and Lord.

4. Rural people should be taught about the beliefs and values of the Christian life and encouraged to apply them in their daily lives.

5. Rural people have a special calling to be stewards of the natural resources God has placed in the world.

6. Worshiping/ministering congregations of Christian faith should be available to all rural people.

7. Policies and practices of the American government and economy have often contributed to personal and community disadvantage in rural America, and these areas of neglect should be redressed through policies geared toward justice and fairness.

8. The old six-mile boundaries of community, the driving paradigm of the settlement period, is no longer functional. The 30-mile (or county) model seems to be emerging; so, we are called to work diligently to form and model new communities.

The rural community of our society is in crisis, as is the entire planet. Repeatedly, one needs to be reminded that within a crisis situation there is opportunity for positive change. The Chinese have a curse that goes "may you live in a time of crisis." The nature of crisis calls the church to stop for a moment to take inventory of what is happening. In this process, the church and all its people can experience the call to serve in the world in order to free it from the threats to its survival. "Such times are also times of transition, invitation and opportunity. The New Testament word for such a time is *kairos*—a time pregnant with possibilities."[2] In rural America, we are at such a moment; and what does the church have to offer?

The church can offer perspective on the moral issues in the crises we confront; we need to make connections between those issues and the choices we confront and make. We must be faithful to a moral vision—what would it mean to fashion an economy and conduct our relationships as if every human being had equal and sacred value?

> The church needs to provide a prophetic spirituality—a spirituality that is true to our core as Christians, one that is not conservative or liberal nor divided along denominational lines. The prophetic biblical tradition is rooted in the Hebrew sages, Jesus, and the early Christian community. Through the centuries it has been expressed by God-called believers who have spoken out and lived out the word of God regarding justice, righteousness, and love. Prophetic spirituality can be found in virtually every renewal and reform movement in history.[3]

We have come to see that the call of Christ to love others as he has loved them mandates that we address the social structures that violate human dignity—it is a call to social justice. As Peter Henriot of the Center of Concern puts it so well: "Social justice means loving others so much that I work to change structures that violate their dignity."[4]

But more. We must call individuals to holy living—shunning sin and acting with responsibility. In the past, Christians often stressed the sinfulness of persons or the sinfulness of social structures and institutions. In truth, sin is found in both, feeding on each other. Sinful people create and sustain sinful institutions; those institutions in turn foster practices that make responsible, holy living more difficult.

The Christian community, like all communities, needs to ask the question, "Why?" Why do we find ourselves in the midst of structures, systems and attitudes that are contributing

167

rapidly to the unraveling of rural communities and the deterioration of the land itself? The Christian community needs to ask still another fundamental question, "Why not?" Why not move onto a more just and sustainable path of development in the years ahead? Why not work for the maintenance of the integrity of creation and the welfare of future generations? Why not invent and maintain a caregiving and renewing society—one in which its sciences, technologies, industries, and economic structures will serve these ends? Today, rural ministry involves the most awesome challenge it has ever faced. Contributing to the settlement of immigrant communities that were planted across the rural landscape of the North American continent was the first chapter in the history of the rural church. The challenge of creating sustainable communities now faces the church in rural areas as it seeks to fulfill its ministry of caring for the land and people.

The reign of God is both next-worldly and this-worldly. It is the "already" and the "not yet." It is the "here" and the "here-after." It is both "within" and "without." The dignity of the human person and the conditions wherein that human person lives, are integrally linked together. What affects one affects the other. Therefore, analyzing the condition of the community becomes important. Asking the questions of why there is not harmony, *shalom*, and right order is what justice and renewal in rural America is all about.

Perhaps we need to look at Saint Paul, his ministry to the Gentiles, for a guide to defining our renewal of rural ministry. Saint Paul defined his mission in terms of the people to whom he was ministering—the Gentiles or non-Jews. In his Epistles, nearly all written to meet the needs of the moment, Saint Paul laid the foundations on which subsequent Christian mission would be built. His ardent devotion to Christ became the center of his preaching and teaching and of his personal faith and life; Paul re-visioned mission in light of the gospel and Jesus' life and words. Paul understood that his own salvation as well as that of others depended on his ability to reach others on terms they could understand. "I have become all things to all people, that I might by all means save some. I do it all for the sake of the gospel, so that I may share in its blessings" (1 Cor. 9:22–23).

Paul's ministry method was simple, yet profound: home visitation and marketplace witness. It included a combination of listening to the needs of the people and building a community to address those needs. Though Paul traveled to many towns, he was able to empower the people in each of those towns to live out their Christian commitment. He literally worked himself out of a job by empowering leaders to minister within their own community, then moving on to do so again.

His social strategy was to call persons to experience the life-changing power of the Holy Spirit (Rom. 8:1–17). They became righteous people who, as they permeated society, changed evil practices and structures, a process that has been a long, slow journey. Pride, sloth and lust have plagued the Christian movement at each step. Simply calling people to be righteous is not enough if the structures tend to pull believers back into sin. Changing the structures is not enough if the people have not been transformed by the Gospel. The battle must be waged on both fronts (Eph. 4–6).

The tradition of mission and ministry that Saint Paul began continued with the Patristic Fathers, who also contribute to the discussion of what re-visioning mission and ministry means today. The era of the Patristics began sometime in the first century. They saw their mission as one of clarification of the Christian faith. But what can the Patristics teach us? They were not specialists; rather they were generalists whose writings give us a sense of the whole, the bigger picture if you will. They were accomplished preachers who knew that the truth had to be spoken or written in an eloquent and convincing manner in order to persuade, to appeal to the heart as well as to the mind. They were masters in the use of imagery and symbolism—a powerful way to articulate a vision of mission. Ignatius of Antioch described Christian life in terms of constructing a building:

169

You are like the stones of the Father's temple, having been made ready for the building of God the Father and carried up to the heights by the engine of Jesus Christ, which is the cross, using the Holy Spirit as a rope. And faith is your windlass, and love is the road leading up to God.[5]

Like the Patristic Fathers, our mission must be specifically rooted in Scripture and tradition, grounded in the reality of this time and this place, and our mission must be risky enough to capture a vision.

The word vision comes from the Latin derivative, *videre*, which means "to see." Vision is about seeing what is, which is accomplished through the medium of eyesight, and seeing what can be, which is accomplished through the medium of insight. Keen eyesight is needed to be grounded in the reality of time and place. Contemplative insight speaks of the sacred voice within. Prophets are visionaries because they possess a combination of both keen eyesight and contemplative insight. Prophets in rural America today are those who contemplate, name, and proclaim the problems, needs, and strengths in rural communities and then dare to articulate a vision or model of how to meet the challenge, on the one hand, while calling for transformed people who live out holy, responsible, loving lives. This vision is grounded in the life and words of Jesus. The whole focus of Jesus' ministry was to proclaim and plant seeds of God's reign on earth: "The time is fulfilled, and the kingdom of God has come near" (Mark 1:15). Religious institutions such as women religious, rural organizations, and rural ministry training centers are some of our modern-day rural prophets—meeting real needs consonant with a re-visioning of mission. In rural America today, at this time and in this place, the congregation or parish is the place where faith meets these challenges.

The need for a renewal in the shape of rural ministry has been suggested. The principles of caring and renewal have been seen as rooted in biblical wisdom and faith. The issues that threaten the health of the land and welfare of rural communities are historically unprecedented in magnitude. Dare we take on the tasks of rural ministry with renewed vision and determination? And how might we do that?

Consider the following examples:

- The Western North Dakota Synod of the Evangelical Lutheran Church of America, under the direction of Bishop Robert Lynne, has initiated an exciting lay leadership program called "Growing in Faith to Serve (GIFTS)." The purpose of this program is to provide a life-long catechumenate designed to train lay persons to be leaders in their congregations. A special emphasis of the program is on developing leadership that sees the community outside its church doors as the mission field, as opposed to seeing the mission field as being in some foreign land. Each lay person who participates in the GIFTS program has a clergy-trained mentor. GIFTS training is divided into three areas: heart, head, and hand. While primary emphasis thus far has been on academic (head) work in the areas of biblical studies, church history, church doctrine, and faith interpretation, GIFTS is currently beginning to focus on spiritual formation and discipleship (heart) training. Interactive video conferences focusing on the development of leadership skills, conflict management, and church meetings that work will round out the "hand" aspect of the program.

- When Leland Heriford retired from an urban pastorate in 1980, he returned to his family home place near Modena, Missouri. The Baptist Church there had fewer than twenty active members. He and his wife began actively and aggressively calling on families. They looked up old friends and made new ones. Today the church is flourishing! About two hundred persons have been baptized into its fellowship. Lives have been changed. So has the community.

171

- In 1980 the Millington Church of God (Anderson) was meeting in a small open country school house with an average worship attendance of six to eight persons. Pastor David Chambers at that time brought to the church his philosophy that "a busy church is aggressive in God's work." Under his direction, the congregation purchased an abandoned church building in the village of Millington which seated 250 in the sanctuary and had fourteen classrooms. The focus of the church's work then became community-minded, an emergency needs program was developed which provided both food and money to needy households. The church affiliated with the local social services office to provide counseling services, money management training, and emergency hospital and dental care. In response to high divorce rates in Millington, support groups for divorce recovery and single parenting were provided. The local Rotary Club was invited to use the church's fellowship hall for meetings. Disciple groups were formed to meet in various geographical areas of the community and a "Fishermen's Club" for men was initiated with a focus on evangelism and outreach. The current average worship attendance of the Millington Church of God is 150 persons.

Recasting the Old Tasks

In this section, we will return to Toffler's three wave typology and attempt some "prophetic" statements about how rural churches in the Information Age will do their work. How can the traditional functions of church life be recast in this present context?

First, there seems to be almost universal agreement that a local church should address about half a dozen basic functions. If a church is not addressing these needs, it should be questioned whether it is indeed about the business of being church. In each religious tradition, these tasks will take a different format, but each should be addressed and in fact is addressed in a vital, growing church fulfilling its Christ-centered mission. These functions are:

- worship
- outreach/witness
- nurture/discipleship
- ministry
- fellowship
- mission

These functions are not discrete. An activity may involve several of these functions. In particular places and times and at specific moments in the life of a church one or two of these functions may receive primary focus. But no one of them should be neglected. Further, some persons are more gifted for leadership in one or two functions than they are in the others. Herein lies a danger. If a congregation "goes to seed" on a single function, it will distort the gospel. Therefore, as one thinks about doing church in the era of the third wave, the design must include all six functions. Take note of the Millington and Modena examples. Which of the six functions do you find? How do you define each of these six in your denomination, church, or congregation? Are all six present in your local church? Which are emphasized? Why? We will return to this in the next major section.

Second, not all churches in the twenty-first century will be Information Age churches. Not all congregations will have moved from first to second wave structures and processes in the twentieth century. Tens of thousands of rural, relational, place churches continue to exist. Often, they fit a segment of the population. Likewise, many second wave programmatic churches will continue on. Choice, of course, is one of the characteristics of the Information Age. Rather than becoming angry with a church for being "old fashioned," it will be more productive to recognize that first and second wave churches will continue to serve the kingdom. The point is that they get the essential functions done. But also recognize that some

173

people will not respond to first and second wave churches. This is particularly true of young, well-educated adults.

Third, those judicatory officers whose task it is to work with the regional configuration of churches will need to come to recognize the importance of "ecclesiological ecology." This means that no longer will the denomination demand that churches be standardized. Because of the diversity of people, a diversity of types of congregations is mandated. The concepts of "designer" and "signature" churches will be explored. These are churches that target specific "people" and "lifestyle" groups within an area. In town and country areas this could mean churches geared to people, who in retirement, have moved from the cities to a small town or lakeside development; pockets of poor folk who are not comfortable in the high spire "Church Street" congregations; service workers whose schedule does not allow them to participate in church at the traditional times and places; and the young adults whose creativity will lead them to "color way outside the lines." This suggests that in a given rural area (e.g., a county) there may be twenty to fifty congregations of five to fifteen denominational identities with several different worship styles, targeting different lifestyle groups for outreach, focusing on specific ministry needs and few, if any, of them seeking to be all things to all people. The key factor in this era of "ecclesiological ecology" is that most of the churches will come to see and affirm their mutual interdependence. No one congregational expression is likely to be able to attract the diverse kinds of persons who will populate rural counties.

Fourth, denominational structures are in trouble. In part, this is because denominational origins reflect issues of another age—theological issues, such as free will/determinism, means of grace, biblical hermeneutics—or ethnic identities which have faded in importance, and socio-cultural identities which are declining in power. In part, it reflects a reaction to the heavy authoritarianism of denominational hierarchy. And in part, it reflects the individualism and independent spirit of the age.

We hope the Information Age will offer new models both for denominational and interdenominational connectionalism, dialogue, accountability, and development. Hopefully, the language of an ecosystem that allows for competition and cooperation and takes note of the importance of interdependence will be included. Perhaps a new form of ecumenism that accepts the fact that there may not be one "best" way for churches, at least for the present, will develop. Specifically, in the body of church lies a place for differences in traditions of worship, ministry, evangelism, and nurture.

Different, but Cooperating

Each particular church's ministry and mission differs within its context. It is the task of the local congregation to identify and carry out its particular mission. However, when seen in the light of the biblical image of the body of Christ, the particular congregation often can best live out its mission in cooperation with other congregations . . . a particular church, working with other congregations, can carry out God's work of saving and renewing rural people and communities.

The Church: Responding to Rural America, a report approved by the 203rd General Assembly 1991, Presbyterian Church (USA)

Fifth, if first wave churches continue to carry some excess baggage of traditionalism and second wave churches are often carriers of some forms of modernity, then the coming of the third wave and the creation of new congregations that fit the new era will offer an occasion to remove some of the barnacles of culture that have so often been confused with the gospel. The need to create new forms of the church will allow a time to return to the mandates and commands of Christ, examine, and re-implant them into current culture. We think that this process will be guided by the six basic functions with which this section began. Hopefully, having learned from the mistakes of first and second wave formulations of the church, the third wave expression will be more faithful to the will of God. (We recognize that it is likely a new set of barnacles will attach themselves to the third wave churches. Then, another round of renewal will become necessary.)

Sixth, contemporary seminarians will find themselves serving first or second wave churches or will be involved in the formation of a third wave congregation. If the former, one crucial decision will be whether to seek to move this congregation to a third wave expression of the church, or to accept it for what it is and serve it. Others will opt for or experience a call to form a third wave church. If so, spend some time in contemplation about how the six basic functions of church might be expressed among a population of third wave persons. Examples might include:

- Store clerks who work on Sunday
- Health-care shift workers
- Lake people, new-to-rural retirees
- Telecommuter professionals and their families
- Craftspersons who want to be involved in a ministry
- Educators who want deep discussion of biblical literature

Seventh, implicit in ministry among third wave people is the likelihood that instead of being "pastor of a parish church," or in addition to that, one may be involved in several different congregational expressions. For example, one clergy couple might be involved in the life of all six of the examples noted in the previous paragraph. This would certainly change the traditional role of clergy. It would mean lots more facilitating, less being the final authority. It would certainly make one more dependent upon the gifts and graces of the laity. One's identity would be more that of a missionary than that of a professional clergyperson.

Eighth, in most instances one will need to deal with the congregation's understanding of its "field." Instead of a dis-

crete six-mile field where it has the "franchise" from its denomination, it will need to become at least a thirty-mile church
that cooperates and competes with several other congregations
both from its denomination and others. Some will try to be like
a Wal-Mart and provide for the larger portion of the population
around. Others will be "designer" churches addressing specific
people or lifestyle groups, and others will discover a "signature" ministry, something they do better than anyone around.
While some six-mile communities have seen their population
depleted, most congregations still can find enough unchurched
persons within fifteen or twenty miles by networking around
a ministry to have a vital role to play in the ecclesiological
ecosystem.

Strengthening Ministry Through Ecumenism

Washington County is nestled along the Ohio River in
southeast Ohio. Marietta, a town of about 15,500, is the
county seat. The population of the entire county is about
63,000. The land area ranks fifth in the state of Ohio. Many
of the major Christian denominations are found in the area.

The congregations of these denominations share at least
one thing in common: all are isolated from their judicatory
offices by at least a 90-minute drive. In addition, there are
many smaller membership congregations of these denominations in the towns and villages around the country as well
as in the open countryside.

The Washington County Ecumenical Cooperative has
worked since 1985 to pool resources among the churches
to strengthen, enhance, and develop the ministries of these
churches, with a special focus on strengthening both the
clergy and lay leadership of local churches. Through the
work of W.C.E.C., it is hoped that congregations will become
involved in ministries which they would not undertake
alone.

In Lowell, for example, four congregations (Highland Ridge Community United Church of Christ, the Lowell United Methodist Church, Our Lady of Mercy Roman Catholic Church, and St. John's United Church of Christ) have joined together in a number of ministries including a food pantry and clothing shop. An ecumenical Vacation Bible School held each summer draws over ninety children from the churches and the community. A cooperative council of laity and clergy helps to oversee the work in that area.

In western Washington County, a group of churches representing primarily Presbyterian and United Methodist congregations have banded together, with the support of the community, to open a food pantry and thrift shop. Meanwhile, the Steering Committee has identified two areas of ministry in which the cooperative will focus in the future: 1) strengthening the individual congregations of the ecumenical clusters, and 2) exploring and implementing ways that the churches in the county can work in the area of economic development.

Appalachia: Signs of Hope, The Appalachian Development Committee of The United Methodist Church, 1992.

Ninth, at the end of the second wave era, one important role for the church to play is in the formation of the new larger thirty-mile community. This development will take several forms. On the one hand, churches in Mighthavebeenvilles need to come to recognize that they are now in a neighborhood within a larger thirty-mile community, not at the center of a vibrant six-mile town. They cannot usually compete program-for-program with the large church in Agraville. But they can either become a rural "neighborhood" church or a church serving the thirty-mile community around a specialized ministry. Examples of these distinctive forms of congregational life might include:

- the country/western music alternative
- center for home schooled families

178

- prayer ministry church
- senior adult ministry church
- boomer congregation
- liturgical alternative

Tenth, town and country ministry in some locations will need to rely more and more on bivocational, tent-maker, and lay ministry. At one time a degree from a seminary was seen as credentialing for a professional position. But because so very many mainline Protestant churches were first wave churches located in Mighthavebeenvilles, which have been losing population for many decades, many churches find themselves unable to "afford" a professional. In the Roman Catholic Church, because of declining vocations to the priesthood, many parishes are served by a part-time priest, a religious, or a parish administrator. One cannot but wonder if one of the reasons that God is calling so many "second" career persons into ministry is that God has in mind the possibility of many of them serving a rural church bivocationally. One may use the other vocation as a vehicle for doing ministry as well, in a place that might otherwise not be able to afford a pastor.

Eleventh, the last century of urban domination of rural life has left a lot of hurt, both personal and environmental, in town and country communities. Ministers in the twenty-first century will have opportunity to address both personal and institutional problems from prophetic, priestly, and pastoral leadership roles. While ministries in the areas of mission and outreach are important and must be addressed, one must be careful not to neglect the other basic functions of the church. Certainly, God has different roles for each one to play, and even these can vary across the course of a career. One must ever be careful to seek the specific will of God concerning both the role and the style of role one is to perform. Just as there is not one best way to do church at this point in time, there does not seem to be one "Christian" role or way to play that role right now.

Twelfth, for the person who desires that his/her life really count, town and country ministry offers much at the turn of the century. Old forms are in decline. New paradigms are emerging. One has the opportunity to shape as well as to be shaped. It is the time of adventure and mission. It is a time for entrepreneurs more than for practitioners. It is a time to express creativity more than learning how to do the routine. Any time of change is difficult. But God is calling the best and the brightest to rural ministry in this age.

New Tasks for a Re-visioned Ministry

Six new tasks are necessary for a re-visioned rural ministry. These tasks are: listening, addressing people's concerns in worship, development of new ethics, building supportive community, providing a prophetic role, and finally, addressing issues of institutional integrity.

Listening The first task in ministry in the rural sector is listening, and raising one's awareness of rural issues. This task unfolds by visiting, hearing, and seeing. Thus, the first thing the new pastor should do is visit and listen to her parishioners. She should also visit community people, not only members of the congregation. This is not only the task of the pastor, however. All members of the congregation are ministers and should listen to each other and thereby gain an awareness of issues affecting rural peoples. Until the problem of rural America and its agriculture and other vocations are clearly defined to include concerns about the welfare of rural community, the farm family, and the health of the land, it is difficult to raise the right questions and to pursue new courses of action.

Ministry involves a constant commitment to problem articulation associated with the raising of the questions that others fear to ask. It is very personal, but it is also social. This is at the heart of Christian freedom—freedom to dare to ask forthright questions. Do we dare ask, "How ought agriculture serve the health of the land, the integrity of rural community, and the future?"

180

Addressing people's concerns in worship Such listening
will lead to the second task in rural ministry, which involves
visioning and especially addressing people's concerns in worship. Are the churches in rural America suggesting a more
holistic definition of life in worship? To what degree are
Christian people helping to define the idea of sustainable or
regenerative community? Worship helps provide a transcendent viewpoint. It gives a "foretaste of the feast to come," a
glimpse of the kingdom in whose light we can assess what is
happening in rural life, and in particular lives.

We need to ask, "To what extent are the churches contributing to new personal and social values, such as environmental
health, resource preservation, good community, and the welfare of the future?" All of these are essential for shifting from
an exhaustive to a regenerative future. Are we moving from the
values of profit to nutrition, from property to home, produc-
tivity to sustainability, bigness to appropriateness, cheap food
to food security, human cleverness to nature's wisdom, from
labor reduction to meaningful labor, convenience to purposefulness, individualism to community, present satisfaction to
welfare of the future?

Developing new ethics Listening and worship can lead to
the development of new ethics. Where do ideas about right and
wrong and good and bad come from? We simply assume that
good agriculture—as with other rural occupations in the
U.S.—means maximized production, that the good life can be
equated with a higher standard of living. We assume that having
more disposable income is good. From the perspectives provided by clear problem analysis and a vision of a more preferred, sustainable future, churches are in a position to offer
insights for new normative constructions with new social and
environmental standards for what might be considered good.
Churches can help form people with a new moral vision.

The responsibility of the church in rural ministry is to
discern God's will. This may mean passing judgment from
biblical and theological perspectives about how to care for the

181

land. As a matter of faith, we must discern what elements of our science and technology, our social, political, and economic life, are in accord with God's will. In addition, many modern-day prophets are speaking about a new vision for rural America. These prophets include some of the following writers, speakers, poets, and visionaries: Wendell Berry, Wes Jackson, Dean Freudenberger, Marty Strange, Ron Kroese, Fr. Thomas Berry.

If our agriculture is not sustainable or enhancing, and if it is not a clear demonstration of stewardship, then it is wrong. If our communities are threatened by greed or hatred or selfishness, we are called to say so and to work to actualize a different vision. In these days of crisis, more than ever before, ministry demands "telling the truth." This is the cost of discipleship.

Building supportive community Underlying every other task is the fourth, the building of supportive community. One of the church's most basic tasks is that of providing supportive community for all. This includes those who relate to the land as keepers and caretakers, or primary producers. The church can convene conflicting parties. It can, and does, encourage farmers to be more interdependent with each other. It can and does promote the formation of coalitions. It can remind everyone (producers, processors, consumers, policy-makers, input suppliers) of the interdependence of creation and all humankind; interdependencies of food and environment, and individuals and their communities.

Land, Church, and Community Project

In order for rural churches to respond to the environmental crisis, a vision of a just and sustainable future must be articulated. Rural churches are in a unique position within their rural community to witness to values of good stewardship and a sustainable future.

182

> The Land, Church, and Community Project, established in 1989, is a project of the National Catholic Rural Life Conference. The project has consistently charted new territory in helping churches manage farmland in a way that reflects good stewardship—both the land and the community. While promoting sustainable agriculture and beginning farmers, the Land, Church, and Community Project creatively heightens the level of engagement of churches within a community of agricultural issues.
>
> Reflecting upon Scripture and tradition is at the heart of the Land, Church, and Community Project. New Melleray Abbey in Peosta, Iowa, has 3,200 acres of farmland. Before engaging in the project, the Trappist monks gave little consideration to sustainable agricultural practices in their farming methods. After articulating a statement of vision, their ministry of farm changed. They now have a full-time farm manager who is implementing the values they espoused.
>
> "The New Melleray Abbey, through our words, thoughts, and deeds, strive by following the Rule of Saint Benedict, to promote the Gospel of Jesus Christ. . . . We believe that the land is a gift from God. It is to be stewarded carefully, in anticipation for the needs of future generations. It is our duty to carefully keep it from harm and help it grow so as to reach a pinnacle of health. . . ; We the members of the New Melleray Abbey, accept this farmland policy . . . to guide our decisions on the use of the farmland we steward."

Providing a prophetic presence We need a church that appreciates all the actors in the rural sector and empowers them to be agents of creative and purposeful change. We need a church that faithfully teaches the scriptural themes of stewardship and justice for all creation. We need a church that reminds everyone that salvation in biblical understanding involves the redemption of all aspects of creation. We need a church that can address the needs of rural community and farm youth and can encourage youth to respond to God's call, in the midst of crisis, to serve for the restoration of the land and rural community. We need a church that can stand with farm workers as they continually struggle for fair wages and safe and decent working conditions.

We need a church that can encourage non-farm people in distant cities to break away from land consuming and wasteful habits. Urban and rural people need an alternative to thinking that cheap food is a basic human right, especially if it consumes the soil upon which the future depends, and if one of its costs is the foreclosure of family farms and the boarding up of communities, including the churches.

Some rural church support networks are now in place. But the need at this time is to learn how to strengthen these networks as they advocate in the public policy arena for the research and development of a mix of activities for promoting sustainable, regenerative food systems that are dependent on healthy rural communities and farm families. Sustainable community, sustainable agricultural technology, and sustainable farm families go together.

Meeting Rural Needs by Re-visioning Mission

Women religious, like rural communities and churches, are revising their mission statements, redefining their ministries, and transforming the role of a sister in today's world. The School Sisters of Notre Dame of Mankato, Minnesota—a women religious community located in a rural town—recently defined their vision of mission to the rural people.

For over one hundred years, they were defined by their ministry of teaching in Catholic schools located in rural towns. Today, either those schools are closed or there are not enough sisters to staff them. Therefore, if they were to continue being true to their historical commitment to serve rural people, it would be necessary to re-vision rural mission and rural ministry. Their rural life committee met the challenge by articulating a vision statement:

"As School Sisters of Notre Dame we commit ourselves to rural people by our presence among them.

We believe all people have the power within themselves to do what needs to be done to preserve the rural community.

The task is to empower one another.

We believe in our connection with the earth. We reverence all creation as a sacred revelation of God. We believe that we need to establish a right planetary consciousness.

We believe that by being immersed in rural life we will rediscover what it means to be rural by the way in which we live among the people of a specific geographic community.

We believe that in the past being rural meant to live a simple lifestyle, practice resourcefulness, reverence the earth, and connect faith to daily life events. It is our hope to re-kindle these values.

We believe that we come to this geographic area as co-learners.

We believe that we will need to discover and help re-define communities of faith.

We believe that healthy rural communities grow out of just distribution and care of the land.

We believe we can help nurture the caring and neighborliness of rural communities."

As a result of this re-visioning of mission, two of their sisters answered the call of their Community leadership to work within the rural diocese of Winona, Minnesota, to find a suitable location to minister and discern the area's specific needs. They believe that serving rural communities is not only important for people, but is also important for the church as a whole as a community of believers.

Addressing issues of institutional integrity The sixth task in rural ministry involves the issues of institutional integrity. We must work for effective levels of interdenominational and interfaith cooperation in the rural setting. People are isolated and alienated enough in rural society. Supporting sustainable agriculture and rural community requires deep respect and cooperation across all of our religious and cultural traditions.

The colleges and seminaries of the churches of this nation, whether rural or urban, have a continual responsibility not only to provide elective course offerings for interested students, but curricular themes that give focus to the vast and complex subject of rural community and agriculture. We must overcome agricultural illiteracy in liberal arts and theological education.

The churches need to overcome, as rapidly as possible, old and bad habits of treating rural congregations only as training grounds for beginning clergy or holding grounds for near retirees. The most gifted people need to be serving at the most difficult and isolated places. Support structures for ministry in rural America today need to be appropriate to need and responsibility. Everyone must work for a higher performance in institutional integrity, particularly when it comes to equitable salary and pension provisions.

Viable Structures for Contemporary Rural Ministry and Mission

It should be obvious that we are convinced that business cannot continue as usual for town and country churches. Just as new ideas and new institutions are needed to address today's rural issues, new structures are also needed if the necessary work is to be accomplished.

Denominational and ecumenical cooperative ministries Cooperative ministries include such structures as the large parish, multiple charge parish, group ministries, federated church, and enlarged charge. As such, these models are not new, having emerged in the early twentieth century. There are two aspects of cooperative ministries, however, that need specific attention today. First, the impact of rural issues as outlined in this book is so large and conceivably overwhelming that they may be best addressed by a coalition of churches instead of lone "Don Quixote" congregations. Second, the history of cooperative ministries suggests that they have the greatest effectiveness when they are initiated with the aid of the laity and sustained with on-going training for both laity and clergy. The lack of on-going training in cooperative ministry results in misunderstandings and even undermining of the cooperative ministry's purposes and goals. Since the issues impacting town and country communities are so critical, nothing will suffice but the best cooperative ministry development and the best on-going support for these ministries.

Rural areas that have experienced significant out-migration may find that ecumenical cooperative ministries provide the greatest strengthening of their ministries. Other options for areas of decreasing population include house churches, fellowships, missions, and base communities.

The Baptist Church in Weed, New Mexico, is an interesting one. Its pastor, David Radcliff, is a balding banjo player. One of his outreach tasks is "The Sacrament! Mountain Boys." This five-piece Western Swing band (including a woman bass player) performs at church and community events. Maxine Radcliff operates the community cafe. There she serves up   salvation and good counsel along with coffee and sandwiches. The monthly newsletter of WBC has become the larger community's newspaper. It includes advertisements from other congregations including ones from the non-institutional Church of Christ.

Possible Cooperative Ministry Structures

Examples of cooperative ministry include the following:

Larger Parish—a number of congregations together using a parish-wide governing board, and other committees and work groups as the parish may determine.

Multiple Church Parish—an intentionally organized group of two or more churches in which each church continues to relate to its own governing board and also participates in a parish-wide council.

Blended Ministry Parish—the merging of the organizations and membership of churches spread throughout a defined geographical area into one church that intentionally develops two or more worship/program centers at agreed upon locations, for which there is one governing body.

Group Ministry—a loosely organized group of two or more churches in which ordained ministers are appointed/hired by each church. The ministry may appoint or elect a coordinator.

Enlarged Charge—two or more congregations, usually on the same circuit and/or relatively equal size, that work as a unit with the leadership of one or more pastors. The churches may share one governing board and set of committees.

Extended or Shared Ministry—a larger membership church sharing ministry with a smaller membership church usually served by one pastor.

Cluster Groups—a group of churches located in the same geographical area with a loosely knit organization which allows the participating congregations to engage in cooperative programs in varying degrees.

Probe Staff—composed of ordained ministers and other staff assigned to a geographic region to explore possibilities for cooperation and developing strategy for improved ministries to persons.

Ecumenical Parish—an ecumenical congregation formed by churches of different Christian denominations.

from *The Book of Discipline of The United Methodist Church, 1992*, revised for ecumenical usage.

Church development and redevelopment models Northern Johnson County, Missouri, like much of the Midwest, has experienced loss of farm-based families during much of this century. Once along a three-mile stretch of highway there lived thirteen families. Today all of them are gone. Several churches have closed while others are hanging on. In the past decade some new, non-farm, families have settled in the area. It seemed that too many barriers existed between them and the old churches. Southern Baptists planted a new congregation about midway on the twenty-mile road between Knobrouster and Concordia. It targeted the young non-farm rural families. In just a few years it was reaching well over one hundred persons and has constructed a very useable church.

Conventional wisdom would have noted the death and decline of congregations in this area. But a missional eye and ear saw and heard a need and opportunity; a new church was formed.

Although recent church development approaches have tended to be focused on suburban areas, a wide variety of church development approaches need to be used in town and country settings as we journey into the twenty-first century. Church revitalization, which focuses on strengthening the present congregation and helping it organize for effective ministry, is one approach. One example of this is United Methodism's NOW(rm) model,[6] which helps smaller congregations to simplify and strengthen their ministries under the basic headings of nurture, outreach, witness, and resource ministries.

The following definitions serve to illustrate the NOW(rm) model:

- Nurture and fellowship focus largely on the internal needs of a congregation and prepare people of that church for ministry outside their congregation within the context of their community and the world.
- Outreach includes: 1) ministries of compassion involving a congregation in addressing the immediate needs of individuals, families, and communities; 2) community ministries of concern and advocacy; and 3) regional, national, and global ministries that call on a congregation to engage the structures and values of society, and to move toward justice and righteousness in public policies.

189

- Witness gives people the opportunity to share their faith understanding of personal and corporate salvation, reconciliation, worship, celebration, spiritual development, and discipline.
- Organization and administration ministries effectively utilize human resources, economic support, facilities, organizational and administrative processes, and linkages with denominational and ecumenical resources.

The United Methodist Church is not alone in recognizing the need for rural church redevelopment. The American Baptist denomination offers its "Seeds of Renewal" training, which is designed to strengthen smaller congregations, including those in rural areas. This training program includes a special emphasis on developing practical responses to changing social patterns and values. Also, in 1991 Presbyterian Church (USA) initiated redevelopment of its rural congregations, with a special emphasis upon cooperating with other congregations. The Evangelical Lutheran Church of America, in 1994, announced a new rural ministry program with regional bases and a national director. It also gave a $600,000 rural development grant to Iowa for church outreach.

Have you been to Branson, Missouri? More than thirty music theaters. Millions of visitors annually. Area Southern Baptists saw a need. A chaplain serves "the strip." A worship service for the performers is held in the wee hours of Wednesday night/Thursday morning. On Sunday 750 to 1000 people worship in one of the theaters. Aren't there other places and opportunities for non-traditional rural churches and ministries?

The Bible announces eternal life for people, not institutions. In the U.S. thousands of congregations have died. Boom and bust towns, change in ethnic make-up of an area, declining population, and poor leadership are among the causes. The concept of hospice might help a congregation die with a sense of "mission accomplished." Components should include a celebration event in which victories are retold, transfer of

190

membership to a neighboring congregation, the disposal of property (hopefully in ways that funds received could be used in missional ways), and debts and responsibilities are addressed. (Many rural congregations have cemeteries that should not be abandoned.) See what policies your faith family has in place for helping a congregation deal with the closure.

The advocacy model of rural ministry   Justice is the advocacy ingredient of Christian rural mission and ministry. Tc do justice is to ask the question, Why are family farm hog facilities economically more viable, environmentally more sustainable, and morally more just than factory farm hog operations? Asking this question and working toward a solution is justice or social change. "Until he has established justice in the earth; and the coastlands wait for his teaching" (Isa. 42:4).

Charity is the direct service ingredient of Christian rural mission and ministry. To do charity is to meet the direct need, the impending need. These might take the form of offering counseling to an embattled farmer, offering a rural family groceries—charity is the first step to justice. Moving beyond charity requires the ability to feel another's pain, which leads to compassion and compassion provokes justice.

A remarkable Hasidic rabbi, Levi Yitzhak of Berdichev in Ukraine, used to say that he had discovered the meaning of love from a drunken peasant.

> The rabbi was visiting the owner of a tavern in the Polish countryside. As he walked in, he saw two peasants at a table. Both were gloriously in their cups. Arms around each other, they were protesting how much each loved the other.
>
> Suddenly Ivan said to Peter: "Peter, tell me, what hurts me?"
>
> Bleary-eyed, Peter looked at Ivan: "How do I know what hurts you?"
>
> Ivan's answer was swift: "If you don't know what hurts me, how can you say you love me?"[7]

Doing ministry in rural communities ought to incorporate both ingredients of Christian mission—providing charity and doing justice. It must meet real needs and challenge the institutions and structures that perpetuate the problems requiring ministry. Who does ministry? The church is the people and through our baptism into the Christian community, we all share in the priesthood of Christ. Therefore, all baptized persons, together with the minister, priest, or parish administrator, have a baptismal responsibility to be active and productive participants in society, and society in return has an obligation to enable them to participate.

Faith-based, congregation-based, and *church-based* organizing are three terms heard today to describe an activism that is grounded in the reality of a place, rooted in the faith of the people, cultivated by Scripture, producing a harvest of justice in the rural community. They differ only in approaches.

The model for church-based organizing contains two criteria: organized people and organized action. The ideal success of church-based organizing is to have an abundance of people with an abundance of gifts to have the power to act on common values. Church-based organizing is built by developing relationships through one-on-ones in churches. The purpose of doing one-on-one visits is to identify people's values and interests, match and enhance the values and interests of leaders, and bring them together to enter the public arena. When those values mesh with the interests of individual churches, people will commit themselves to action. Once relationships are developed based upon values and interests, then churches come together to impact issues in the public arena. Building community and promoting community does make sense in rural towns, but creativity is needed to recapture that inherently wonderful quality. Church, often the only official institution remaining in a small town, is in a unique position to foster sustainable rural communities. That's why church-based organizing can be effective—it integrates faith with justice, builds community and leadership within a town. Church-based organizations bring together congregations from a variety of denominations to work together for community change.

Transformation and the Renewal
of the Rural Church

Transformation is a scary word. How does it happen? To each of us, it happens in different ways. Dorothee Soelle says that "when she came to understand Auschwitz, she joined the peace movement. What she was saying is that she did not want to rid herself of God like many people who hand responsibility over to God alone. Rather she realized that what God needs is us in relationship, in order to realize what was intended in creation. God dreams us, and we should not let God dream alone."[8] Transformation is a powerful word. For Rosa Parks, her transformation came from not giving up her seat on the bus. For some, transformation comes with the birth of a child. For others, it is the loss of a farm or mine. For another, it is seeing a homeless person on the street. Whatever, it is coming to the realization that God needs us; in fact, God calls us to realize what was intended for all of creation.

In the renewal of rural church, what we need right now is community. When we come together to access the common good based upon Jesus' call to come follow me, "we form a prophetic spiritual network—a network that crosses the lines of race, class, gender, region and political parties. This prophetic spiritual network can act as the midwife of new possibilities."[9] Many are calling this network communitarian; we can look at it as answering the questions—who is my neighbor and what kind of community do I want to live in? We have the power to answer those questions. We have the power to choose our neighbors and our community. What we need to do is recognize that power, accept it, and answer Jesus' call to come, follow me.

CHAPTER NINE

Living Out the Vision: Clergy, Laity, and Congregational Action

Now that we have articulated the vision for rural ministry that we understand to be emerging from many rural congregations, we see that it is really a re-vision of the old, old vision that began with Genesis and continued with Jesus Christ and Paul and now continues with us.

Christian Scriptures show that the church of first-century Christianity was really many local communities, each with its own physical environment, distinctive make-up, beginnings, and particular problems and challenges. Preaching and teaching took account of the culture of each audience. Jesus told stories that related to rural people's way of life. He followed or broke rural social customs to convey his message about the Reign of God. Saint Paul, on the other hand, sometimes spoke to rough urban dock workers and at other times educated urban elites. In every case the vision of the Reign of God was articulated in a way that communicated with persons within their local culture.

In similar fashion, we turn to the practical question of how the local rural congregation and its pastor or priest can live out Christ's vision in a way that speaks to the local rural context. How can we do the work of ministry? How can the pastor or

194

priest, the laity individually, and all of them corporately live out and communicate the presence of God?

Our perspective is that it is the entire congregation that does the work of ministry. The clergy person and all the members of the laity are part of the corporate body that works collectively. One image that is particularly appropriate for the rural congregation is Paul's metaphor of the church as the organic body that, when all its parts are working together smoothly, builds itself up in love (Eph. 4:15; 1 Cor. 12:12–31). Although the majority of this chapter is devoted to considering the work of the pastor or priest and also to the work of the laity, it is clear that it is the *interaction between clergy and laity* that builds up the body of Christ, the local congregation. It is exactly this interaction in a system that is the cutting edge of ministry studies today; we will return to it at the conclusion of the chapter.

The Rural Context as Cross-Cultural

Before we begin to lay out the different roles of pastor and laity, it is important to understand the rural context in the United States as in many ways a cross-cultural experience. In his work on rural children, *Migrants, Sharecroppers and Mountaineers*,[1] Dr. Robert Coles speaks about the feeling for geography found in the drawings of young people. Children who grow up in rural areas depict animals, vegetation, landscapes, trees, and sky with people and houses as a unified whole. Suburban children and urban children, by contrast, depict the natural elements as decorations or additions, not integral elements. Rural children experience and understand nature and human life differently from urban children.

Similarly, in writing his biography of Lyndon Johnson, Robert A. Caro found that he had to live in the Texas hill country and come to understand its culture and mores before he could understand Lyndon Johnson. "When the postmistress in Johnson City, Texas, said to me, 'You're never going to

understand Lyndon Johnson unless you understand the land,'
I remember thinking 'this sounds like a Grade B Western! What
does she mean, 'The land?' ' "

But Caro learned "the land" by moving to the edge of hill
country and living there. Eventually the city boy learned. The
chapters in Caro's first volume, *The Path to Power*,[2] which dealt
with hill country life, are among the finest portrayals of that
subject. It was by getting close to the land and its people that
Caro learned the local culture. He moved, through experience,
from a city consciousness to what was for him a cross-cultural
consciousness, Hill Country Rural. We are suggesting that
immersing oneself in rural culture and consciousness is an
essential avenue into ministry.

Had Robert Caro been a missionary, he would have sought
the contours of God's self-communication within the land and
people of the Texas hill country. In doing so, he would be able
to engage in a conscious exchange between his own Christian
self-understanding and that of the local culture. Local settings,
languages, knowledge, and values are the context for immer-
sion in rural ministry. As a feature of contemporary Christian
nurture, it is vital to the Christian charge to bring the Gospel
to every culture. Doing so with sensitivity involves distinguishing between the culture and the religion. Nevertheless, if God
is active and present in every culture, as we believe, then it is
important to be able to see God operating in and through local
life and culture. While we must be careful not to impose forms
of Christianity born in one culture or among one class of people
on cultures where it is foreign, it is always possible to ask how
God is speaking in the local vernacular. Where is God here?
What is God doing here? How can we best carry on ministry
here?[3]

Rural Culture as a Cross-Cultural Experience

Pastoring a congregation in rural America is often greatly different from pastoring an urban or suburban congregation. There are even significant variations between rural settings in different parts of the country. This is why it is important for you to consider and understand the particular context in which you serve.

If you did not grow up in rural America or if it is something you perceive yourself as trying to escape, you may be tempted to view rural American culture as something negative. Remember, however, that what is at issue is the culture of a particular group of people. Granted, it may be a culture different from your own. However, rural America has institutions, values, rituals, behaviors, signs, and symbols which are meaningful to its people.

Therefore, it may be helpful for you to think of yourself as being in a cross-cultural experience. A cross-cultural experience in Africa, Asia, or Europe would afford you many educational opportunities. What, therefore, can you learn by living in rural American culture? What are its values, institutions, behaviors, etc? What do they mean to the people?

from *The Rural Ministry Primer* by Deborah K. Cronin

The Plunge into Rural Ministry

Every study we have seen suggests how important it is that the clergy person competently and conscientiously carry out the traditional tasks of ministry: leading worship, preaching, pastoral care, and leadership. How these are best carried out in rural communities differs with each location. One generalization that holds true is that the ministry needs to address community. Rural pastors must find ways to engage their ministries and lives with the core of the rural communities they serve. This is absolutely central to effective rural pastoral ministry and can no longer be seen as an option. All too many rural churches have been the victim of pastors who were "just passing through." The goal of pastoral ministry in the rural setting must now move away from the pastor being perceived as a religious professional on an upwardly mobile career track to that of becoming a pastor to the rural community.

> Our priests and ministers, for the most part, are very good when it comes to "churchy" matters. They provide good liturgical leadership, good leadership in religious education, good leadership in reaching out to people in need of word and sacrament. But one of the unfortunate realities of our small rural communities is that many of them are without effective leaders. I do not mean that priests and ministers should be the primary solvers of problems, not even the primary ones righting social wrongs and injustices. But it seems to me that seminarians should be taught to be conveners of people, leaders enabling the people to be the "principal agents" in the pursuit of justice and in the pursuit of economic development.[4]

Engagement in a rural community means becoming part of that community and learning to value both its strengths and its peculiarities. Engagement in a rural community means finding out where the local folks gather to talk politics and nonsense, as well as participating in the various celebrations, rites of passage, and duties that are important to the community. Engagement in a rural community means putting down roots with the expectation of living ten to twenty years in that community, if not a lifetime.

Effective rural pastors today cannot merely be spectators in the communities they serve. They must be participants in those rural endeavors where their own particular gifts and graces are most needed. This may range from serving as a volunteer fire fighter to coaching Little League baseball to serving in political office. All of these activities, of course, imply a theology of active presence. When physical and emotional needs surface in the community, quality involvement may require providing care, support, and problem-solving and also require addressing the root causes of suffering. An example of this is pastors who organize community groups to respond to crises caused by natural disasters, and to remedy the lack of affordable housing, food, or medical care.

All this does not imply that rural pastors need to function as "lone rangers." In fact, just the opposite is a true reflection of rural communities, where the willingness to reach out and help one's neighbors is considered a strong virtue. Rural pastors need to seek allies to strengthen and inform their work. School teachers and administrators, local government officials, and such agencies as the office of aging, human resources, public health, and farm and environmental organizations provide resources that a pastor needs to know and call on in rural America. This interaction with other agencies and resources becomes another means by which the rural pastor ministers in community life.

The Many Roles of Rural Pastors

Churches in rural towns or open country settings offer pastors the opportunity to assume a variety of vitally important roles, all falling under the stated or implied job description of "rural pastor." We will describe a number of these roles, knowing that the special combination of them that a rural pastor is expected to play differs from one community to another, from one congregation to another, and sometimes differs even within a congregation at different times.

The success of your ministry in a given rural community may very well depend upon how well you and the appropriate laity come to a common understanding of what roles you will play and in what order of importance you will attend to them. It is important for Protestants to negotiate this issue openly and explicitly at the outset of a pastor's tenure in a parish. For Roman Catholic priests and other clergy, correspondingly, it may be crucial to seek out lay feedback and evaluation. It is also true that expectations may change over time or that they will need to be renegotiated for a time. For example, pastors whose counseling load becomes overwhelming during certain times may need to be explicit about the fact that their worship leadership is less creative during those times. They could then seek lay feedback on how to proceed in terms of role adjustment and how to sort out priorities.

Failure to clarify expectations can also have humorous consequences. A clergy friend tells of arriving at a rural Kentucky church, his first pastorate out of seminary, a half-hour before the fellowship dinner welcoming him was to begin. He warmly greeted the women in the kitchen who were putting the finishing touches on the meal. They shook hands with him and said, "The coffee isn't yet made." He nodded and went out to greet other parishioners as they arrived. Soon a lady from the kitchen pulled on his sleeve and said, "The coffee isn't made yet." Brock commented that it should be made soon, because it was not long before time for the meal to begin. Eventually a delegation of women from the kitchen came to Brock and said, "The coffee isn't made and we don't know how to make it. Our previous pastor [who had been with them for twenty years] *always* made the coffee!" The role of pastor as "coffeemaker" was up for negotiation.

In rural congregations "quality" is often defined in terms of getting more than you expected. Pastors will find that going beyond the expectations of their congregation will almost always have a powerful, positive effect on their ministry. If expectations have been significantly surpassed in one area of ministry, difficulties in other areas may be forgiven more quickly. Steve was helping the moving company unload his family's furniture into the parsonage of his new parish when an older couple stopped by to see him. They were concerned because the elderly mother of the wife was in the hospital and not expected to live much longer. They asked if someday soon he would visit her. He assured them he would. With the moving van still in the driveway and the furniture not yet unloaded, he went to the hospital to visit a dying woman he did not know.

Before Steve had even preached his first sermon from the pulpit, the sermon his actions had preached had gotten around the entire congregation. Favorable evaluations of the new pastor abounded before most parishioners had even met him.

1. The Rural Pastor as Shepherd and Community Chaplain The "pastor" role model brings to mind the shepherding images found in the New Testament. Jesus said that the good shepherd is one who knows her flock and is known by them (John 10:2–4, 14). The shepherding image, of course, is a familiar one to most rural communities. Incorporated into this role is also the activity of listening, since rural peoples, by nature a story-telling people, appreciate pastors who will listen to them. When the rural congregation senses that the pastor listens to them, understands them, and truly cares about them, then this role can be enacted with effectiveness.[5]

One of the chief joys of rural ministry is the possibility of forming deep, long-lasting, and intimate relationships with parishioners and with members of the community. The rural pastor learns quickly that pastoral care is not given only by pastors, but by a whole network of relationships throughout the church and community. Within this relational web, visitation takes on increased importance. In short, there is a high expectation in rural congregations that their pastor will effectively care for the well and be there to bury the dead. That is, the pastoral care aspects of rural ministry are extremely important.

There is still ample opportunity for the pastor to drop in on parishioners and their families at their homes. The pastor who keeps a pair of coveralls and "muck boots" in the trunk of her car will still be welcomed to climb aboard the combine or climb into the livestock pen to rub shoulders with a parishioner. With more persons carrying on dual employment, and commuting outside of their county to work in industrial or service sector jobs, finding people at home becomes difficult. Even visiting people in their work places can become a challenge. Increasingly, rural pastors are turning to the telephone to set up appointments to visit with people either at home or in the work place. One rural pastor in Oregon discovered that he could do effective pastoral care over the telephone, calling people early in the morning before they left for work, or catching them in the transition times just before supper or after the ten o'clock news.

"Marrying and Burying Well"

Rural congregations expect that their pastors will participate in all types of family events, such as birthdays, confirmation receptions, wedding rehearsal dinners, and occasional family meals. Rural pastors need to work hard to get to know people so that they will be able to "marry and bury well." Moreover, in general they should not wait to be asked or invited. If the volunteer rescue squad takes a member or friend of the church to the hospital, the rural pastor should proceed to the emergency room as soon as possible. If the rural pastor, while in the coffee shop, hears of a death, she should go to the deceased's home at once. Presiding at a wedding or funeral without going to the reception or funeral meal is considered rude in most rural communities. The expectation is high that the pastor will be there, pray well, and care well. The statement "Adversity came and the pastor showed up at the door," is a rural compliment of highest regard. If this kind of intimate involvement in the rural community's life represents unfamiliar ground to rural pastors whose own background is urban or suburban, then finding a pastor with a strong and effective tenure in rural ministry to serve as a mentor and guide may prove helpful. The basic rule is: "Be there and don't wait for an invitation."

Another privilege of the rural pastor is being able to function as a chaplain within the community as a whole. This is done in many ways but primarily through involvement in the life of the community. For example, those who suffer some accident or other adversity often find themselves the recipients of aid on a community-wide basis. A pillar of the community may suffer a stroke and find that his health insurance covers only a fraction of his costs. In the effort to raise money to help him out, the pastors in the community are simply expected to pitch in. This involvement may also take the form of participating in local service organizations, networks of helping professionals, or the local ministerial association. One Nebraska pastor discovered that he made more ministry contacts for pastoral care by serving on the volunteer fire department than he ever made while on official church business.

It is in this setting that the importance of funerals in rural communities comes to the fore. It is often the custom for all adults that are able to attend a resident's funeral—banks and small town businesses close; farmers leave the fields. Even if the deceased was not a member of a local congregation, a pastor of one of the local churches may be asked to perform the service. Unless one's denominational polity precludes officiating at a funeral for a nonmember, the rural pastor will do well to think of this service as a very significant opportunity to serve a much wider network of persons within the community than just his/her own congregation. This ministry of sharing the gospel in an active and caring way at a time of widespread grief and pain in a community has often been such a significant event that the future ministry of the pastor who performs the service has been either very positively or negatively affected.

Other occasions of public prayer offer similar opportunities to position oneself as chaplain to the community. Even praying over the chicken at the seed company dinner or the Rotary Club should not be treated lightly.[6] Subtle choices of language can make a difference in how persons who are now strangers consider the possibility of approaching a rural pastor when in need. In addition, references to local history during public events speak volumes to rural congregations and communities about the commitment and pride of the pastor.

Experience teaches many rural pastors that the ecumenical community is a vital resource for the shepherding or chaplain role. In rural communities, the whole population is often affected by the same experiences, whether it be weather, a tragic accident, or a change in the local economic situation. The gathering of pastors and laity of all of the churches in the community to talk about the common needs of persons can bring forth creative and effective strategies for offering the care of the Christian community to those who seldom, if ever, darken the doors of a church building.

Involvement in the ministerial alliance also allows the rural pastor to share the burdens of community chaplaincy with other pastors and helps avoid burnout.

The Importance of Listening

One way rural pastors can show that they are truly listening to their congregations is by paying attention to "rural speak," i.e., the special words of the rural community's vocabulary. Consider the following:

Rural congregations have vocabularies that are unfamiliar [to outsiders]. For example, while "bail" to the urban person may mean getting someone out of jail, "bale," to the rural person refers to measurement of hay. In everyday speech these terms can be confusing to the new rural pastor.

Other categories of vocabulary which may be new and unfamiliar to the rural pastor include words describing agricultural equipment (plow, combine, disc, etc.), livestock breeds (Charolois, Holstein, Angus, etc.), geographical descriptions (cove, swale, bench, etc.), and mining techniques (drag line, pit, pillar and post, etc.).

New rural pastors need to take the time to listen to these new vocabulary words and decipher what they mean to their parishioners.

The Rural Ministry Primer by Deborah K. Cronin

---

2. The Rural Pastor as Worship Leader The role of pastor traditionally includes being the leader of worship, and rural congregations certainly expect their pastors to be competent in this respect. They also long for worship services that will acknowledge, celebrate, challenge, explore, and even lament the day-to-day events of rural life. Churchgoers bring their questions, fears, and desires to worship, in the hope that God, through worship and pastoral leadership, will address issues that are part of their lives and community context. The lectionary contains many texts that focus upon rural life and issues. These may be interwoven with sermons and liturgical materials that lift up current rural themes. Rural America contains a treasury of traditional rural sacred music, including both texts and music styles, which can add authenticity to the rural congregation's worship experience. For example, one church includes an occasional congregational hymn accompanied by a bluegrass quartet consisting of amateur musicians from that congregation. This perennially well-received musical offering puts the congregation in touch with their rural roots and provides a platform from which to explore contemporary rural issues.

Preaching is an important aspect of worship for most rural congregations. Statistics show that while most mainline churches are located in rural areas, many and often the majority of their pastors come from urban areas. Consequently, these pastors need guidance in preaching messages and stories that convey a sense of contextual reality to their congregations. Stories that have been told for one or two generations (and sometimes longer) often explain why the present generation thinks, speaks, and acts as it does. This is why some of the most effective town and country theme sermons are grounded in story-telling.

"People with a rural background," writes Cronin, "feel empowered and derive spiritual meaning from sermons illustrating Jesus' teachings and using rural symbols."[7] It is helpful to remember that Jesus was a country boy, born in a barn in Bethlehem, and raised by a laborer in the small town of Nazareth. From the stories he told we know that he understood the language of seeds, barns, animals, and fishing. Rural listeners better understand Jesus when rural pastors illuminate the meaning of these stories through their preaching. If some of these sermons also prophetically lift up the important rural issues of our day, such as poverty and good stewardship of the land, then so much the better.

Also important to worship leadership is the role of music in the service or Mass. If there is an organized choir in the church, the pastor can be grateful; choirs tend to be wonderful support and fellowship groups. However, the emphasis in rural congregations might best be on congregational participation. The ensemble of a few voices can function as a teaching choir, more than a performing choir. They could serve to teach new hymns to a congregation; they could also lead a congregation in singing in rounds and in antiphonal response (men—women; pulpit-side—piano/organ side). Even one person with a strong voice can do a lot to assist a willing congregation to praise God in song and can help a congregation learn to enjoy that.

Roman Catholic parishes are being encouraged to have two or three people with good voices serve as cantors teaching the congregation responses. This may be a very appropriate pattern for many rural churches, especially small churches with no possibility of an organized choir. In many parishes cantors sing the verses of hymns and the worshipers sing the chorus; that is also a good teaching pattern.

Another item, significant beyond the attention it will receive here, is the place of youth in the worship service. Involving them as leaders of worship in serious and ongoing ways signals their importance to the congregation and it encourages their development as future leaders in the church. It also encourages the congregation to see their youth in these roles and suggests that all the members of the church could assist in worship.

While the role of prayer in worship as well as personal devotions is vital to increasing courage and remembering the source of our power, the place of the Pastoral Prayer or the Prayers of the People is special in rural congregations. This prayer is an essential place for lifting up local concerns—prayers for those who are losing jobs in the factory closing, those who are ill or in other pain, those losing their farms, bankers and businesspeople hurting, concerns about the school, and so forth. This is often the place where pain can be legitimately lifted up, said out loud the first time, and marked as a Christian concern. In some ways praying is a way for the pastor to hang out a shingle, suggesting a concern for issues like alcoholism or declining business in town or domestic abuse or gay and lesbian issues. It gives parishioners "permission" to speak about such issues in church or in other contexts later if they have heard such concerns offered to God in prayer.

3. **The Rural Pastor as Evangelist** Another model for rural pastoral ministry to be explored is that of evangelist. The notion that all rural people have a church home is not true. Furthermore, the work of evangelism is incorporated in the pastor's role as community chaplain and missional leader.

Certainly evangelism *per se* should be on the agenda of the rural pastor. However, since rural society tends to be highly relational in nature, the evangelism model of "showing and inviting" will usually prove more authentic and, thus, more effective than "telling" evangelism efforts. Bear in mind, too, that evangelism in rural areas needs to be just as sophisticated as that practiced in urban and suburban areas, even while it is intrinsically different. It may be helpful for rural pastors to understand the sociology of generational theories (retirees, babyboomers, baby busters, generation X) and master usage of the "information highway." (On the latter, see Appendix B).

4. **The Rural Pastor as Missional Leader and Change Agent** Kennon L. Callahan (author of *Effective Church Leadership: Building on the Twelve Keys*) and others have written about the development of a "churched culture" within U.S. denominations. Persons involved with established churches have tended to develop an insider culture with its own lan-

guage, customs, and rituals. It is easy for such cultures to substitute religion for spirituality and church work for Christian discipleship. Such "churched culture" has had ample time to develop in many rural churches. There it tends to take the shape of a concern for the survival of the church.

The rural pastor finds herself in a strategic position to address this subtle and long-standing development. Because he or she is usually an "outsider," the rural pastor brings to the church a broader perspective on the emergence of new mission fields at the doorsteps of our churches. To be a missional leader at the close of the twentieth century is to aid the leaders of the congregation to discern what God is doing in our world and in this place today. Rather than simply maintaining the church, rural congregations are being called to mediate God's grace in their locations and to develop ways to nurture themselves and their communities spiritually and holistically.

This often means that the pastor is called to initiate the process of change with the congregation. Said one rural pastor, "These people won't change! Every time I offer a new idea it seems to fall to the floor with a dull thud. How can they expect the church to develop or grow if they aren't willing to change?" Yes, it's true; sometimes rural folks, like others, are slow to change and somewhat set in their ways. However, they are generally not opposed to change that proves valuable. The frustrations experienced by the pastor quoted above were deep and real, but unnecessary. Upon examination, the pastor realized that he was bringing to the situation his assumptions and perceptions that were formed in an urban culture. Once he calmed down and began to seek understanding of his people and their ways, he discovered that they would indeed change, if led in a way consistent with their local culture.

Pastors seeking change in rural churches would do well to remember that it is *the process* of initiating change that is most important. The pastor should remember three principles:

a. *Lay the foundation* If the pastor is perceived as an outside threat, local leaders may "circle the wagons" to defend against the threat of change; after all, many changes have been experienced as negative and painful in the last two decades of rural life. If, however, the pastor has taken time and effort to be "adopted" into the folk society of the church and community, then the pastor can begin to lead for change. The pastor can be effective if the process of change is consistent with that congregation's culture.

b. *Seek input and permission to try the change for a set amount of time* Rural people like to experiment with or "try out" a new technique or way of doing things. Consultation with selected professionals and people in the parish is essential to initiating any change. Extension, other clergy, and these professionals in the community can advise the pastor about what processes for change have tended to work and which have not.

c. *Give the congregation an opportunity to evaluate the change* The pastor must be open to following the desires and opinions of the congregation. Probably the biggest "crunch point" for the pastor is the pace of change. One must remember that most rural cultures are formed by natural organic processes. As Smokey the Bear has said, "Trees take time." One rural pastor's sanity was saved by the wise counsel of a neighboring experienced pastor who said, "You want things to change? Give it time." In most rural communities, that is not a bad guideline. If the change works well, the congregation will generally support it.

5. The Rural Pastor as Counselor and Social Worker Not very long ago, the rural pastor often found himself or herself to be the primary local resource for meeting human and social needs of community members, especially in more remote communities. Specialized resources, such as those addressing spousal abuse or chemical addictions, could be hard for local persons to access.

Fortunately, useful resources and networks of helping professionals have been expanding in recent years. However, the role of the rural pastor as counselor and social worker is of high importance.

It is vital that the rural pastor get as much training as possible in the analysis of social needs, in techniques for providing effective help, and in making referrals. This is especially true in the areas of family violence, child abuse, alcoholism and chemical dependency, suicide and its prevention, and grief processes. This training can be found through continuing education programs from seminaries, hospitals, county social service agencies, or public educational institutions such as land grant universities or area community colleges.

It is important that the pastor not exceed her or his limits of competency. When moving into a rural community, the wise pastor begins a search for helping resources in the area.

Contact with county social services, other public and private helping agencies, special programs offered by hospitals and clinics, and other professionals in private practice should all be explored and professional acquaintances begun. These relationships enable a pastor who knows the community to make referrals of persons who need specialized care.

Many rural people frequently drive several miles to purchase specialized goods and services. For personal or family counseling they will likely *not* be willing to receive that service locally. It is, therefore, important for a pastor to meet the providers of those services in nearby communities. The importance of this cannot be overstated. The effective rural pastor will seek out and develop relationships with persons to whom he/she would feel comfortable referring beloved parishioners.

The rural community offers another possibility for the rural pastor's helping work. Often, there are laity who are in positions to offer helpful care and resourcing through their daily work. In one small town, the proprietors of the local general store often encountered people with a variety of personal, social, and economic needs. The local rural pastor discovered that by sharing what he learned in his continuing education with these storekeepers, they were equipped to better encounter those who came through their store and shared their needs while paying for their groceries. The pastor was also able to provide a list of referral resources, including names, addresses, and phone numbers, which the storekeepers could use in directing people to helping agencies and resources. Establishing a working relationship with the school superintendent and principal and local veterinarians may also have a similar payoff. These professionals have wide contact with a variety of residents and can often spot and identify ministry needs before such needs ever make it to the door of the pastor's office.

6. The Rural Pastor as Prophet The role of the rural pastor as prophet is fraught with difficulty. The close and long-lasting nature of relationships in rural communities can produce an incredible sense of solidarity among people. Add to this the breadth and depth of kinship networks and family loyalties, and the calling of the prophet can demand skills and diplomacy far beyond the reach of most of us. When considering that God usually calls prophets to proclaim God's judgment upon current situations and announce a new vision of a preferred future for the community, the prophet can be in the position of challenging current power arrangements, positions of status and privilege, and a status quo supported by the vested interests of some groups within the community. As Jesus warned, "Prophets are not without honor except in their own country and in their own house." (Matt. 13:57).

In a sense, the prophet is called to ask, "What does God see when God looks at our community and at our church? How would God feel about what God sees, based on our understanding of God from the Scriptures? Would God want to do anything about the current situation? If so, what is our role as God's people in initiating change?"

The rural pastor/prophet needs to nurture a sense of the "big picture" of the larger society and the global realities surrounding the community. One problem faced by local communities is their need for reliable information about who they currently are, how they are currently changing, and what larger societal forces are at work influencing their possibilities for life.

One issue faced by the rural pastor is the question of who speaks for God and when. Pastors need to be clear when they are speaking with the authority of their pastoral position and when they are expressing their own opinion.

If rural pastors are to respond to the call to serve as prophet, they will be well advised to sharpen their conflict management skills. Prophets must realize that any leadership for change in the rural community will bring forth conflict. The issue is *how* the conflict will be addressed and managed. To facilitate the resolution of conflict, utilizing appropriate ground rules and conflict resolution techniques can be a valuable service and ministry to a rural community.

One of the most challenging aspects of rural pastoral ministry is deciding which pastoral role is appropriate at what time in the life of the community. Since rural America tends to take years to warm up to newcomers, the roles of pastor/listener and teacher are usually most appropriate at the beginning of a pastorate. The problem, however, is that drastic changes—often negative in nature—have impacted rural America in recent years. These, of course, call for prophetic and administrative responses. Pastors who sense the need to engage in prophetic and administrative ministries early in a rural pastorate must be sure to build support and consensus for these ministries with the laity. One way to initiate this foundation is through the use of community forums, which allow the rural community to lift issues that demand immediate response from the faith community. Another way is to encourage members of the church who are fully aware of pressing needs to present them to the congregation for their response. Once again, the style the pastor should seek is never that of the "lone ranger," but rather that of pastor/listener/teacher/evangelist, and, yes, prophet, who understands the power of the community to speak the truth when given the opportunity and the encouragement.

Continuing Education
and Other Supportive Networks

If we are to expect rural pastors to stay in rural communities for a period of ten to twenty years, or even for a lifetime, then they will require meaningful support for both their ministry and their individual lives. One way to provide support is simply for denominational judicatory leaders (area ministers, bishops, presidents, executives, district superintendents, etc.) to say it is okay for a pastor to do this. In other words, the expectation that pastors will first serve in smaller, rural congregations and then move up the denominational corporate ladder to larger urban and suburban congregations must cease to be the measurement by which effectiveness in pastoral ministry is determined.

Other means of support for rural pastors and their households include insuring that there will be adequate time and funding for vacations, continuing education, and study leaves. Educational experiences that afford the pastor the opportunity to learn more about rural sociology and rural ministry are crucial. Focus events such as those sponsored by the Rural Chaplains Association, an ecumenical group of clergy and lay persons committed to rural ministry, and on-going educational events such as the Rural Social Science Education program offered by Texas A&M University are outstanding examples of such experiences.

Finally, rural ministry training and continuing education for pastors should include developing competency in current telecommunications technologies. Isolation has traditionally been one of the biggest factors negatively impacting rural pastors. Separation from useful resources has also been a problem. Use of such telecommunications as Internet, e-mail, and information services can be extremely helpful to the rural pastor serving in a geographically isolated community. (See Appendix B.)

Another consideration is providing denominational funding for rural pastors to help reduce educational debts, particularly since rural churches tend to pay less than their urban and suburban counterparts. Currently the United Church of Christ offers such a program; the expectation is not that the pastor will make a life-time commitment to rural ministry.

Support for Pastors in Rural Ministry

The Rural Chaplains Association is established to assist those women and men who sense a call from God to minister in churches, projects, or institutions located in open country, isolated areas, villages, and small and large towns. The Association provides opportunity for Rural Chaplains in The United Methodist Church and other Christian denominations to develop, enhance, and refine their skills of ministry and to participate in a network for fellowship, encouragement, and the sharing of resources and ideas.

Finally, it should be noted that equitable salary programs (i.e., denominational salary supplements) have generally proven ineffective. Too often they become a crutch that allows the local congregation to limp along with neither hope nor the will to heal permanently. At best, they tend to promote dependency, as if small rural congregations did not have the resources to provide for their own ministries.

Discerning God's Will for Today's Laypersons as Individuals and Congregations as a Whole

As with the clergy, the question of their role is relative to rural congregations. What is God's intention for rural communities today? Surely it cannot be the loss of viable economic activity that is so rampant. God's intention cannot be the continued out-migration of natural resources and the pollution of our sources of water. Neither can it be continued tolerance of pastors who would rather be serving some urban or suburban church. What does God want **for** rural communities? Perhaps that question can best be answered by determining what God wants **from** rural congregations.

New models of rural ministry are emerging throughout the country. These models share common threads of values: they are collaborative, often interdenominational, always faith and tradition based; they connect people's experience to their faith; and they are dynamic—because they are born of a faith that does justice. *Faith-based, congregation-based,* and *church-based* organizing are terms heard today to describe an activism that is grounded in the reality of a place, rooted in the faith of the people, cultivated by Scripture, producing a harvest of justice and hope in the rural community. They differ only in approaches. Common to all church-based organizing (described in Chapter Eight) is a building of relationships.

Why build relationships in a rural community? Isn't community a given? These values, if they are to be preserved, must be nurtured in new ways. Community cannot be taken for granted anymore in rural towns. The coffee shop is closed; a self-serve gas and grocery chain is now on the corner of Main and State Streets. Mom and Dad both commute fifteen miles daily to jobs now found only in larger towns or cities. A few senior citizens are cooking food for the church funerals; young mothers bring packaged desserts and processed foods.

Building community and promoting community do make sense in rural towns, but creativity is needed to recapture that inherently wonderful quality. Church, often the only official institution remaining in a small town, is in a unique position to foster sustainable rural communities. That's why church-based organizing can be effective—it integrates faith with justice, builds community and leadership within a town. Church-based organizations bring together congregations from a variety of denominations to work together for community change.

St. Andrew's, a small neighborhood Lutheran congregation located in East Carnegie, Pennsylvania, is one congregation that has a fifteen-year track record of church-based organizing. Pastor Beth Siefert tells her story:

From the beginning, I knew the history of the congregation's involvement in community outreach efforts and the situation within the community. Immediately upon my arrival we sought out and continued our involvement in the evolving effort of our denomination to provide a mission strategy for the area congregations. It was in early 1981 that these efforts led to the formation of an ecumenical church based organization for the training of clergy and laity in community organizing strategies.

Getting to know the people in our community was a priority. We approached this task by seeking out the networks that already existed in the area—local volunteer fire department, local businesses, schools. We established contacts through a series of interviews. From there we found the informal networks that operate in the community—card clubs, golf clubs.

Through our interaction with the people we were able to identify issues that were important to them. Over the years we have organized the community to tackle a number of issues:

- Summer recreational needs for the children of the community
- Blocked development of a go-kart track
- Monitored a local land-fill operation
- Establish a community festival day

Confronting the problems within a local community is one approach to church-based organizing. Another approach toward seeking economic justice is to confront the unjust structures, the institutions. The Sheboygan County Interfaith Organization (SCIO), a congregation-based community organization in eastern Wisconsin, developed a strategy for confronting Kraft/Philip Morris and Pizza Hut/Pepsico, the biggest food conglomerate and largest pizza maker. Jay Klemundt, organizer for the effort, shares his experience:

SCIO teamed up with Sinsinawa Dominicans, the Oblates of Mary Immaculate, other Catholic religious communities, dioceses, and denominational offices through Interfaith Center for Corporate Responsibility (ICCR). With ICCR's

216

networking help, SCIO promoted a serious dialogue with
top Kraft management and the filing of shareholder resolution on dairy pricing and the Cheese Exchange was voted
upon at the Annual Meeting of Kraft/Philip Morris. Both
Kraft and Pizza Hut are scrambling to polish images and to
prop-up sales.

Bible Study and Community Mission

Renewing Rural Iowa, a program for accompanying
churches in renewal through Bible study and community
mission, is a faith-based organizing program across denominational lines. The initiative is funded and developed
by the United Church of Christ, Presbyterian (USA), Episcopal, Evangelical Lutheran Church of America, Christian
Church (Disciples), and The United Methodist Church in
cooperation with PrairieFire Rural Action of Des Moines,
Iowa. American Baptists and Roman Catholics are also
active participants. The results have been phenomenal. Lay
participants have been given a new-found personal confidence and inspired commitment. Pastors are experiencing
a renewal of creativity in their work. Congregations find
their lay leadership more inspired and effective. Communities have been positively impacted by long-needed change
in the functioning of schools, city government, economic
development, and problems of drug and alcohol abuse.

The ministerial association of Ringgold County, Iowa, felt
compelled to write a statement on the corporate hog issue.
This action came directly out of the Bible study. Pastors and
parishioners alike are seeing how factory farming is ripping
faith communities apart, eroding the fabric of the family
farm system of agriculture, and destroying the beauty of the
rural landscape.

The church has a political ministry within society. Christ
serves as our model of political ministry. The Jesus of the
Gospels clearly engaged compassionately with the people he
encountered, no matter what the political ramifications of his

actions. Jesus' mission was to proclaim the reign of God, bringing good news to the poor and freedom to the oppressed. The manner of his execution, by crucifixion, was reserved for political criminals, and therefore it is plain to see that Rome perceived him as a political threat. Yet, Jesus also rejected any attempt to assume earthly power. Christ was political in a faithful way, and faithful in a political way. He was concerned for the whole person, body and soul. This led him to take public stands against injustice just as it continues inevitably to lead rural people into political action.

Rural denominations throughout the country, for example, joined together in common action to impact the 1995 Farm Bill. The Campaign for Sustainable Agriculture that over five hundred diverse groups joined is a network offering concrete proposals of hope for the sustainability of family farming, our food system, and rural communities. This campaign is made of groups who recognize their diversity but affirm their common allegiances and work together.

Using the model of diversity, what can *congregations* or parish leaders do to bring about awareness of food issues, practically and interdenominationally, in their community?

1. Offer community forums where urban, farm, and rural people talk about their self-interest on issues concerning food safety and security.

2. Provide dialogues or retreats where people can talk together about stewardship of the earth in relationship to their faith.

3. Promote Soil and Water Stewardship Week events and resources. For example, plan an interdenominational prayer service for a good growing season.

4. Offer Vacation Bible School classes on farm issues.

5. Have local farmers doing sustainable agriculture give witness talks or reflections on how their faith impacts their farming practices.

218

6. Invite local, state, and national legislators to a listening session of their constituency.

A Question

How would the American rural church appear to the local community if, instead of presenting a small group of people intent on institutional survival, it was viewed as a force for community strength and change? What would this say to the community about Christian discipleship?

A New Vision of Lay Ministry

The need for vital lay ministry has never been stronger. By vital lay ministry we mean lay people who are willing to address the most difficult and challenging issues of their communities because they believe that God is very much interested in the well-being *(shalom)* of those communities. We believe that denominational judicatories must emphasize that congregations have as powerful a role in vital rural ministry as do pastors.

An integral key to vital lay ministry is laity training. In recent years mainline denominations have provided solid laity training in the areas of financial stewardship, lay speaking, biblical studies, Christian education, and the objectives of a wide range of local church committees. While these offerings are helpful and useful, lay persons in town and country churches also need training in transformative, community-based leadership. This includes training aimed at understanding their context. While they may actually live in a community that is impacted by United States policy, especially rural development policy (or lack thereof), they may not have the tools they need to fully identify, describe, critique, and address these issues. It is essential that such training include strategies for identifying and organizing the gifts of congrega-

219

tional members and community residents for enacting needed changes.

It is equally important for rural lay persons who are members of churches with small membership to receive training in effective ministries for that size congregation. This kind of training provides two things smaller rural congregations need: 1) input about "what works" in churches similar to their own, and 2) the self-esteem which comes from recognizing that there are church effectiveness experts who think this size congregation is important.

The increased use of lay ministers and second career pastors in many denominations is to be celebrated. However, it is equally important to provide on-going support and training for these pastors.

In 1994 the Center for Theology and Land surveyed one hundres rural congregations that had been identified as exemplary, vital churches. Asked what factors contributed to their vitality, only one item (of eighty-eight) was found "indispensable" by a majority of respondents. Seventy-two percent of the participants indicated that lay leadership was indispensable to the congregation's energy and drive. The item next-most-frequently indicated as indispensable was only 49 percent—a 23 point gap.[8]

This level of importance makes it all the more surprising that we know so little about the optimal clergy-laity relationship. Perhaps, if Loren Mead is right, we are in the midst of a clergy paradigm shift and our research and experience have not caught up with the change from seeing clergy as the quarterbacks and wide receivers to seeing them as coaches. This shift underscores the significance of learning how clergy can assist laity in God's empowering work, and vice versa. We understand some things about how that is done but are only now turning to the question.[9]

Some of the insights that are emerging are these: Clergy are themselves perceived as members of congregations and cannot stand apart from the system that includes laity. Power resides in the interaction between people whose involvement is strengthened by having genuine influence over some aspect of the system. Clergy can develop leaders and can help build community. One practical way of doing this is by encouraging laity to think about the ministry of their congregations. Congregational studies are useful to this end.[10] The final insight, and one that is vital for the rural church to implement in congregational life, is this: Working together, clergy and laity can have far greater impact on their communities than by maintaining a division of labor that is now anachronistic. Rural congregations know this and are beginning to enact it. That is the shape of the renewal to come; that is where the Holy Spirit is moving.

EPILOGUE

This book initiates a new beginning. It can be looked upon as a call to renewal for the church. As forcefully and imaginatively as possible, the authors have pointed to uniquely new opportunities for rural ministry. What is at stake is the land, the human community, and the future. What is being suggested is that in many rural places the church is the only remaining significant center of community. Being in this position, more than ever before, the church has a prophetic role to play. The church was the center of rural community during the European settlement of rural America. In spite of massive demographic and industrial changes, it continues to be at the center. But the issues are different, requiring more aggressive and imaginative ministries.

The challenge is to continue nurturing Christian congregations, to be a prophetic voice in the community, and engage in the public arena of discussion. The hope is that the church can demonstrate that believers, holding different views, can talk with each other as redeemed people in redemptive ways. One of the causes of violence is said to occur when people are unable to talk with each other. Today the church is called to be a place for reconciling discussion, especially among different income classes. The authors of this book were in conversation for four years. They represent the ecumenical spectrum of the church located in almost all regions of rural America. The process was arduous, but productive and enriching. It is one that we covet for everyone.

The question has been raised from the very beginning of this book: can the church make a difference? Our basic assumption is that the church exists for the world, rather than for itself. The church functions as an instrument of God's redeeming activity in history. The working thesis of this book is that a compelling theological and biblical vision is central for the renewing mission of the church. Vision results in the recognition of the need to re-think theology and ethics in order to re-shape priorities and provide a tool for judgment about the realities of our time. Without a clear and well-informed vision, the status quo remains unchallenged.

Visioning begins with the question: what ought to be? What is God's will for creation both now and for the future? Visioning calls us back to renewed biblical study and theological reflection that embraces the whole creation and its future. The question emerges: why have a vision? The response is simply that where there is a faulty vision, the people perish . . . and so does the land. The authors have noted in their discussions that those who define the situation also define the agenda for action. Vision functions as a goal, a guideline, and a basis for evaluation and judgment. The vision of this book is for a welcoming, healing, and growing church, giving witness to a broad definition of social justice and healthy community. In our time of growing populations and other pressures on the environment, the Christian goals of justice and healthy community assume inter-species justice as well as the welfare of future generations. Thus, the idea of sustainability becomes inseparable from the idea of justice. The development of a renewing and redemptive ministry depends upon a compelling vision. This we have long observed in the Gospels—a vision of God's reign on earth as in heaven.

In the chapters reviewing the history of the growth of the rural church in America and the description of new types of rural churches that have emerged in recent years, it has been suggested that there are few historical precedents to help envision rural ministry for the years ahead. The chapter on moral issues and principles has pointed to long-term challenges that face us today and tomorrow. Past experience, in the face of new issues of historically unprecedented magnitude, does not necessarily equip the church for the type of reconciling ministry that challenges the church of today. This book points to promising models of ministry that describe ways to work to actualize a more just and sustainable society where issues of stewardship are seen in wider perspective. These models demonstrate what is at stake when there is a willingness to take risks by listening to what rural people are saying about stewardship and social responsibility for community and land. It is challenging to take seriously the wisdom and deep concern of marginalized people located in distant places!

This book underscores the importance of rural people, the land and community. The fact that rural populations are changing has been emphasized. As the church is caught up in these changes, the future shape of ministry is pondered. Denominations are beginning to recognize once again the importance of rural ministry. Rather than using rural ministry as a starting point from which one moves to something bigger and better, rural is becoming a place where people will be called for longer service in proclaiming the word, in witnessing, and in mission. In view of the challenges now being faced in the rural sector of society, the best and the brightest need to be positioned in the most needed places. As a matter of justice as well as missional strategy, rural clergy must be compensated equitably with their urban/suburban counterparts. It is a myth that the real cost of living is lower in rural areas and that the work load of rural clergy is lighter. Like our mission support organizations, we need highly skilled people blessed with a clear vision of what God wills for the whole creation to be of service in the most difficult and demanding places of ministry.

In the future, rural ministries will need to be more ecumenical in nature. Ministry will need to be focused more on the entire community and the empowerment of congregations for the renewal of the communities and the land. Seminaries must be more intentional in providing orientation for rural ministry, even in the face of demanding curriculum. Seminarians, lay and clergy leaders all require continual support by their judicatories in providing experiences for enriching the process of visioning responsible futures. One aspect of the process will be the emergence of multi-cultural congregations now that rural America is experiencing the influx of new people. The emphasis in all training and support for rural ministry will be focused on how the churches, still at the center of rural community, can make a contribution in reshaping the future.

Rural ministry is set in a place where one sees quickly that making a difference is possible. The church is still a place of wisdom and transformation. It is located in places where economic and technological power has a tendency to dominate and to trample people, life and land, and where there is little sense of welfare for the future.

Need we remind ourselves that Jesus was born in a dusty barn, in an obscure and distant village? Yet the world was changed. All things are made new.

As was true throughout our history, the rural church is composed of congregations of lay and clergy who are involved in all aspects of the work-a-day world and who are shaping the future in promising ways. How we together care for the land, for the whole of creation, and for community within our locales *and* around the globe will determine the future of civilization. The stakes are high. Let not the church be overcome by the forces of change or despair. Rather, let the promise of the living Christ prevail during these times of awesome challenge.

And the people say:

Amen.

Thirty Questions About a Rural Community

To be effective in a town and country community one must learn about its history, its peoples, its structures, its everyday life, its expectations for pastors, its hopes and fears, and the place of the churches. This list is not a questionnaire one would ask congregational leaders to fill out or write down answers. Nor is it an interview schedule to be given in a single setting. Rather, it is suggestive of some topic areas around which one can engage community residents over several months as opportunity presents itself. Over time one can come to experience a sense that he or she is at home in this place.

Your Place as a Place and its People

1. How did the community come to be? What was the founding dream? What was the covenant upon which the community was built—utopia, commerce, resource exploitation, safety, freedom, or the good life? Where does it now fit in Sim's typology?

2. What is its focal symbol—courthouse square, grain elevator, mine tipple, or some other image of community function?

3. What is/are its chief economic function(s): farm trade, marketing, mill or factory, fishery, timbering, governmental service, recreation/retirement, college, transportation, bedroom community, or institution? Often this is integrated with the dream and the symbol.

4. Who are the honored, the despised, the loveable characters, and the "marginal" people of the town?

5. What world views, values, and norms inform everyday life? What do people in your place believe about—Time (e.g. past, present, or future oriented)? Nature of people? Interpersonal relations? Purpose of activity? Character of nature and the supernatural? (A study of *Ministering Cross Culturally* by S.,G. Lingerfelter and M.,K. Meyers [Baker, 1986] can be very useful in identifying world view issues.)

6. What cultural/racial/ethnic groups are present in the community?

7. What are the barriers that separate people/groups of people: race, religion, education, social status?

8. What are the sins/hurts of the community: the loss of an industry, a disastrous flood, a lynching?

9. What has become of its sons and daughters? Often people and communities in decline feel vindicated by the success of the children in the larger world.

10. What is the people's perception of the place; awareness of other's perception of it?

11. Does the community have distinct "sub-communities"? In a larger small town, some folks will not attend a big "first" church for social and cultural reasons.

12. What seems to be the future of the community—its dreams, who is responsible for dreaming/implementing?

13. In sum, what is the "story" of the community? You need to know and appreciate the story of the community. You need to come to "own" it and become a part of it, because for good or ill, you will.

Your Place as Process

1. What are the magnets of the community? What places, activities, and events draw people?

2. What is the rhythm of everyday life? Daily, weekly, seasonally, annually?

3. What are the corridors/patterns of movement around the place? When can one "pastor" at the coffee shop, the post office, the ice cream parlor, and the sale barn?

4. How are decisions made? Who are the power brokers? Who are the major "get things done" people in the town? What is the route or career path to leadership positions?

5. What are the "routines" of everyday encounters/conversations: greeting, teasing, conducting business, courting, making requests, leave taking? What are the taboos?

6. How do people make a living? What is the routine/rhythm of their work?

7. How does the community relate to other communities in its region—dominance, conflict, subordination?

8. When, where, and how do the residents play? What are the annual events?

9. How does the community assimilate new people?

The Place of Your Church in the Place

1. What role does your church play in the place—leader, cooperator, secondary? Dominant, denominational representative, or distinctive?

2. What kind of reputation does it have—friendly, aloof, rich, middle-class, poor, formal, ordered, informal, loving, conflicting, combative, community-serving, self-serving?

3. What is the relationship between your church and the other congregations in the community?

4. What community resources are available to assist your church in doing ministry?

5. What ministries, programs, events, and activities in the community receive the support of your church?

6. What community leadership roles are filled by active members of your church?

7. How does the community relate to your congregation? Embraces, holds at a distance, rejects?

8. Does your church seek to serve or to dominate the life of the community?

Computer Communication and Rural Ministry

Betty is the pastor of a geographically isolated rural UCC church in the Midwest. She entered the ordained ministry following a twenty-year career as an administrative assistant to the dean of students in a small college. She is widowed and her grown children and grandchildren live some distance from her present home.

During the first two years of her present pastorate Betty was lonely. Her loneliness shrouded her like a dark, heavy, foreboding veil. And then Betty went "on line." That is, via a modem (telephone line communication) attached to her computer, she linked up with an "e-mail (electronic mail)" network. For a nominal charge each month, Betty is now able to use her computer to communicate daily with a lectionary study network, a pastor prayer network, and a network devoted to discussing issues and ideas for rural ministry. Betty has not met the other pastors with whom she communicates via computer and she probably never will. However, her computer colleagues have become her strongest support group and she looks forward to their daily conversations.

Today's rural pastors need to be computer literate. While we may think of rural America as still being that quiet place where only the rural mail carrier, television, and local newspaper offer communication opportunities, that bucolic vision is both outdated and simply not sufficient for the highly technical age in which we live. A large number of previously urban laypersons have moved their businesses, consulting firms, and other service-oriented enterprises to rural communities. Here they have combined living the rural lifestyle with continued professional effectiveness by using computer networks, facsimile machines, and computer software designed to help them transact business hundreds and even thousands of miles from their clients. There is much that today's rural pastors can learn from this model.

A great deal of software has been designed to assist both congregations and pastors. For example, "Concordia Computer Software: Ministry Information System" is specifically designed for churches with small membership. This software enables smaller congregations to keep track of membership records, financial contributions, and accounting. Contact: Concordia Publishing House, Computer Products Department, 3558 South Jefferson Ave., St. Louis, MO 63118–9968, (800) 325–2399. Other denominations offer similar programs.

ECUNET is a telecommunications network used by many Christian denominations. Pastors and laypersons can discuss a wide variety of cultural and church-oriented topics using this network. Contact: 800-RE-ECUNET (800) 733–2863.

An excellent resource that includes easily understandable descriptions of such technical computer terms as "hardware," "software," and "output devices," as well as a wide variety of software systems usable in churches, is found in *Making It Work: Effective Administration in the Small Church* by Douglas Alan Walrath (1994, Judson Press).

Another electronic device that increasing numbers of rural pastors are finding indispensable is the cellular phone. Cellular phones are "wire free" and communicate via a series of antennas and satellite hookups. They allow the rural pastor the flexibility of being able to place telephone calls from one's automobile (where rural pastors spend lots of time!) and also provide a safe way to contact emergency services in remote rural areas.

AUTHORS

Pegge Boehm, PBVM

A Presentation Sister from Aberdeen, South Dakota, Sr. Pegge Boehm is currently enrolled as a Master of Divinity student at St. John's University, Collegeville, Minnesota, after having worked with the National Catholic Rural Life Conference. Research Assistant to Dr. Bernard Evans, the perdue of the Virgil Michel Ecumenical Chair in Rural Social Ministries, she seeks to surface pastoral leadership models in rural parishes with a supporting theology.

Deborah K. Cronin

District Superintendent of the Olean District, New York, United Methodist Church. She has pastored a federated American Baptist-UMC church in Busti, New York, and directed the Western Small Church Rural Life Center in Filer, Idaho. A pastor, writer, and church consultant specializing in town and country and small church ministry, she has authored *The Rural Ministry Primer* and *O for a Dozen Tongues to Sing*.

Gary E. Farley

Taught sociology at Carson-Newman College and Oklahoma Baptist University, 1965–1984. He pastored bivocationally for fifteen years. From 1984–1997 he directed the Rural Church program of the Home Mission Board of the Southern Baptists. He is the Associational Missionary of the Pickens County (Alabama) Baptist Association.

C. Dean Freudenberger

A United Methodist clergyman and Professor of Church and Society/Rural Ministry at Luther Seminary, St. Paul, Minnesota. He writes from the perspective of experience in church and Peace Corps agricultural programs in more than thirty countries over a period of forty years. He is the author of three books and numerous essays and journal articles. His current interests are in the field of agricultural and environmental ethics.

Judith Bortner Heffernan

Executive Director of the Heartland Network for Town and Rural Ministries, United Methodist Church, Columbia, Missouri. She is perhaps best-known for her work on the effects of the farm crisis and the churches' response. Active in the Rural Sociological and other societies, she lectures nationally and internationally. A farmer herself, she is interested in the consequences of changes in the global food system for rural congregations and communities.

Shannon Jung

Director of the Center for Theology and Land, an outreach ministry of the University of Dubuque and Wartburg theological seminaries. The Center trains pastors and supports rural congregations and communities. Dr. Jung has been the pastor of two rural Presbyterian churches; taught theological ethics at Concordia College, Moorhead, Minnesota; and has written *Rural Congregational Studies: A Guide for Good Shepherds* (with Mary Agria) and *We Are Home: A Spirituality of the Environment.*

Sandra A. LaBlanc

Associate in Ministry with the ELCA and called by the Southeastern Iowa Synod to her position as Communications Director of the National Catholic Rural Life Conference. She has held this position for fifteen years, edits *Catholic Rural Life* magazine which has won thirty-threenational awards, has produced videos, audiotapes, and edited liturgical materials. She was raised in a small Iowa town and believes that rural is a "state of mind."

Edward L. Queen II

Senior Research Fellow and Director, Religion and Philanthropy Project at the Indiana University Center on Philanthropy. A former program officer at Lilly Endowment, he has helped to develop several projects on rural ministry. Edward is a church historian by training and the author of *In the South Baptists Are the Center of Gravity: Southern Baptists and Social Change* and co-author of *The Encyclopedia of American Religious History*.

David C. Ruesink

An elder in the Presbyterian church, Ruesink joined the Texas Agricultural Extension Service in 1968. Director of the Rural Social Science Education program (an ecumenical continuing education program for both laity and clergy in the U.S. as well as Canada), he also teaches courses on rural ministry at the Austin Presbyterian Theological Seminary.

NOTES

Chapter 1

1. Genesis 1:12; 2:7, 18, 21, 25, 31; Psalm 104; Job 38–41.

2. Genesis 1:26–30; 2; Psalms 8; 97:1–2; 99:4.

3. Genesis 8; Hosea 2; Deuteronomy 4:26; 30:19; 31:28; Jeremiah 4:23–26.

4. Proverbs 8.

5. Martin B. Bradley et al., *Churches and Church Membership in the U.S. 1990* (Atlanta: Glenmary Research Center, 1992).

6. Lester R. Brown, Nicholas Lenssen, and Hal Kane, *Vital Signs 1995: The Trends That Are Changing Our Future* (New York: Norton, 1995), 118.

7. See Garry Wills, "The New Revolutionaries," *The New York Review of Books* 13 (August 10, 1995), 50–55.

8. Michael Kinnamonn, ed., *Signs of the Spirit: The Official Report of the Seventh Assembly* (Geneva: WCC Publications; and Grand Rapids: Eerdmans, 1991), 54–71.

9. For example, see John Paul II, "And God Saw that It Was Good," Message for the 1990 World Day of Peace (December 8, 1989), *The Pope Speaks* 35:3 (1990), 200–206. For a pastoral statement of the National Conference of Catholic Bishops, see "Renewing the Earth: an Invitation to Reflection and Action on the Environment in Light of Catholic Social Teachings," *Origins* (December 12, 1991).

10. It is quite true that there are many rural communities that are growing. Examples of this include: communities located within commuting range of metropolitan areas; recreation and retirement centers; and towns where large businesses have decided to locate. See "The Rural Rebound," *American Demographics*, May 1994.

It should be noted that even in those rural communities where change is bringing new opportunities for economic renaissance, the landscape and social structure of the community will be altered. Farmers and rural residents forced off their land by urban encroachment or recreational developments often experience depression in ways similar to that experienced in depopulating and declining communities.

11. See Shannon Jung, *We Are Home: A Spirituality of the Environment* (New York: Paulist, 1993), Chapter Four, which makes the case that seeing the world as God's home is in keeping with the witness of Scripture and tradition.

12. For a more detailed discussion of the changes occurring on a national level with churches, please refer to Loren B. Mead's book *The Once and Future Church*, (Washington. D.C.: Alban Institute, 1991). See also his follow-up, *More Than Numbers: The Way Churches Grow*, 1993, and *Transforming Congregations*, 1994, also from the Alban Institute.

13. From an unpublished manuscript, "A Profile of Rural Churches," by Sandra A. LaBlanc (National Catholic Rural Life Conference, 1994).

14. For more information about rural churches, please refer to Br. David G. Andrews, ed., *Ministry in the Small Church* (New York: Sheed & Ward, 1988) or Kent Hunter, *The Lord's Harvest in the Rural Church* (Kansas City: Beacon Hill, 1993). It is important to note that local communities are more and more connected to the wider society and often include a group who have recently moved into the rural community.

15. Peter Drucker, *The New Realities* (New York: HarperCollins, 1990).

16. A few of those farms and organizations that are participating in the Church Land Trust Project are New Melleray Abbey Farms, Peosta, Iowa; the farms of the Sinsinawa Dominicans, Sinsinawa, Wisconsin; and the farms of St. John's Abbey, Collegeville, Minnesota.

Chapter 2

1. For a general discussion of American religious history see Sidney Ahlstrom, *A Religious History of the American People* (New Haven: Yale University Press, 1972); and Martin Marty, *Pilgrims in Their Own Land: 500 Years of American Religion* (Boston: Little, Brown, 1984).

2. For a discussion of nineteenth-century American Protestantism see Robert Handy, *A Christian America: Protestant Hopes and Historical Realities*, rev. ed. (New York: Oxford University Press, 1984); and Martin Marty, *Righteous Empire: The Protestant Experience in America* (New York: Dial Press, 1970).

3. For general histories of Roman Catholicism in America see Jay P. Dolan, *The American Catholic Experience: A History from Colonial Times to the Present* (Garden City: Doubleday, 1992); John Tracy Ellis, *American Catholicism*, rev. ed. (Chicago: University of Chicago Press, 1969); and James Hennesey, *American Catholics: A History of the Roman Catholic Community in the United States* (New York: Oxford University Press, 1981). For John Ireland and Roman Catholic rural communities in the upper Midwest see James M. Moynihan, *The Life of Archbishop John Ireland* (New York: Arno, 1976); Marvin Richard O'Connell, *John Ire-*

land and the American Catholic Church (St. Paul: Minnesota Historical Society Press, 1988); and James P. Shannon, *Catholic Colonization on the Western Frontier* (New York: Arno, 1976).

4. Samuel S. Hill, ed., *Encyclopedia of Religion in the South* (Macon: Mercer University Press, 1984); Charles H. Lippy, *A Bibliography of Religion in the South* (Macon: Mercer University Press, 1985); Charles W. Ferguson, *Organizing to Beat the Devil: Methodists and the Making of America* (Garden City: Doubleday, 1971); William Wright Barnes, *The Southern Baptist Convention, 1845–1953* (Nashville: Broadman, 1954); Edward L. Queen II, *In the South Baptists Are the Center of Gravity: Southern Baptists and Social Change, 1930–1980* (Brooklyn: Carlson Publishing, 1991).

5. Charles Hayward, *Institutional Work for the Country Church* (n.p., 1900).

6. Merwin Swanson, "The Country Life Movement and the American Churches," *Church History* 46 (September 1977), 358–73, and James H. Madison, "Reformers and the Rural Church, 1900–1950," *Journal of American History* 73 (1987), 645–68.

7. Gill, an ordained minister, had co-authored with Pinchot a book on rural churches in Vermont and New York. Brunner was the head of the Moravian Brethren's rural life work, Wilson the Presbyterians', and Vogt the northern Methodists'.

8. For the record of this conference see Paul Vogt, ed., *Church and Country Life: Report of the Conference Held by the Committee on Church and Country Life Under the Authority of the Federal Council of Churches of Christ in America*, November 8, 1915 (New York: Federal Council of Churches, 1916).

9. W. E. B. DuBois, *The Negro Church: Report of a Social Study Made Under the Direction of Atlanta University*; together with the *Proceedings of the Eighth Conference for the Study of Negro Problems* (Atlanta: Atlanta University, 1903).

10. See Ralph A. Felton, *The Study of the Rural Parish: The Method of Survey* (New York: n.p., 1915); *Our Templed Hills: A Study of the Church and Rural Life* (New York: n.p., 1926); *The Church Bus* (Madison, N.J.: n.p., 1946); *A Hundred Games for Rural Communities* (Madison, N.J.: n.p., 1947).

11. David S. Bovee, *The Church and the Land: The National Catholic Rural Life Conference and American Society, 1923–1985* (Ph.D. diss., University of Chicago, 1987); Raymond Witte, *Twenty-five Years of Crusading: A History of the National Catholic Rural Life Conference* (Des Moines: National Catholic Rural Life Conference, 1948).

Chapter 3

1. In 1992 a PBS series (twelve one-hour shows) was aired that visually underscored these verbal images. It is very well done. In most

instances, copies can be borrowed from the library of your state land grant university. The title of the series is *Rural Communities: Legacy and Change*. The videos are supported by a rural sociological text written by Cornelia Flora and others. All of the material is sensitive to the role of the rural and small town church.

2. These, of course, are the themes that Reinhold Niebuhr was sounding in the middle quarter of this century. The arguments of *Moral Man and Immoral Society, The Nature and Destiny of Man, The Self and the Dramas of History*, and other of his writings still ring true.

3. Bradley et al., *Churches and Church Membership*.

This is the third in a series of publications (1972, 1980, and 1990) in which many of the denominations reported church membership by counties across the nation. Because the Glenmary Order of Roman Catholics has played the key role in this effort, it is popularly known as the Glenmary report. Currently it is housed in the International Office of the Church of the Nazarene and directed by Rich Houseal. He has been very helpful in providing the statistical information found in this section.

4. For documentation of these assertions, review Richard Houseal and Dale E. Jones, "A County By County View of Religion in the U.S.," *1993 Yearbook of Churches in the U.S. and Canada* (Nashville: Abingdon, 1993), 11–15.

5. Alvin Toffler, *The Third Wave* (New York: Bantam Books, 1980.)

6. Richard Lingerman, *Small Town America* (Boston: Houghton Mifflin, 1980).

7. Don Dillman, "Social Issues Impacting Agriculture and Rural Area as We Approach the 21st Century," *Rural Sociology 50* (1985), 1–26.

8. Cathy Tyebett, *Under God's Spell* New York: Harcourt Brace and Jovanovich, 1989). See also C. B. Goodykoontz, *Home Missions on the American Frontier* (Caldwell, ID: Caxton, 1939).

9. Kenneth Scott Latourette, *The Great Century: Europe and the United States* (New York: Harper and Row, 1941).

10. Carl S. Dudley and Doug Walrath, *Developing Your Small Church's Potential* (Valley Forge: Judson, 1980).

11. Carl S. Dudley and Sally S. Johnson, *Energizing the Congregation* (Louisville: Westminster/John Knox, 1993).

12. (Princeton: Princeton University Press, 1958).

13. R. Alex Sim, *Land and Community* (Guelph: University of Guelph, 1988). See also his *Plight of the Rural Church* (Toronto: The United Church Publishing House, 1990).

Chapter 4

1. R. Alex Sim, *Land and Community*.

2. Joel Garreau, *Edge Cities* (New York: Anchor Books, 1991).

3. G. Scott Thomas, "Metropolitan America" *American Demographics* (May 1989).

4. Walrath, and Dudley, *Developing Your Small Church's Potential.*

5. Particularly recommended is the study of Wendell Berry, *The Unsettling of America: Culture and Agriculture* (New York: Avon, 1977). See also Cornelia Flora et al., *Rural Communities: Legacy and Change* (Boulder: Westview, 1992).

6. Alvin Toffler, *The Third Wave* (New York: Bantam, 1980). See also his *Power Shifts* and *Future Shock.*

7. Kennon Callahan, *Effective Church Leadership* (San Francisco: Harper and Row, 1990) and *Twelve Keys to an Effective Church* (San Francisco: Harper and Row, 1983). See also Loren Mead, *The Once and Future Church* (Washington. D.C.: Alban Institute, 1991).

8. Leonard Sweet, *Faithquakes* (Nashville: Abingdon, 1994).

9. Alan Bird, "The Rural Heartland in the 90's," *Choices* (Second Quarter, 1990).

10. See Wendell Berry, Wes Jackson, and Bruce Colman, *Meeting the Expectations of the Land* (San Francisco: North Point, 1984).

Chapter 5

1. Even in the regions of the country where plantations and large royal land grants created different economies at first, eventually the family farm system of agricultural production became the norm. This was true in the South and to a lesser extent in the California valleys.

2. Those states from west to east were: California (65), Nebraska (56), Kansas (68), Oklahoma (67), Texas (173), Minnesota (90), Iowa (98), Missouri (102), Arkansas (50), Wisconsin (78), Illinois (80), Michigan (59), Indiana (72), Ohio (79), Kentucky (108), Tennessee (106), Alabama (58), Georgia (54), Virginia (59), and North Carolina (82). *American Bankers Association Mid-Year Survey*, October 1986.

3. In the spring of 1985, at the request of the U.S. Congress's House Committee on Agriculture, Professors William D. Heffernan and Judith Bortner Heffernan (rural sociologists at the University of Missouri) conducted a study of families that had lost their family farm during the previous five years solely for financial reasons. The high levels of depression and despair reported by the farm couples interviewed surprised mental health professionals who had helped design the questions for the personal interviews. Every woman and every man except one admitted to becoming depressed in the course of losing their farm. Two-thirds reported withdrawing from family and friends; almost three-quarters admitted to experiencing feelings of worthlessness and becoming restless and unable to concentrate; and three-quarters of the men and over half of the women experienced difficulty with sleeping. Among other significant findings were reports of experiencing great changes in moods (67%

men, 81% women); of becoming confused (54% men, 31% women) and admitting to becoming "more physically aggressive" (29% men, 31% women). These data are cited in many places including the following: William D. Heffernan and Judith B. Heffernan. "Human Cost of the Farm Crisis," in Joseph Molnar, ed., *Agricultural Change: Consequences for Southern Farms and Rural Communities* (Boulder: Westview, 1986).

4. It is important to cite a few examples. The *Interchurch Ministries of Nebraska* organized support for and initiated a crisis hot-line. Later, in response to a growing need, they developed with the support of the state legislature a farmer/lender mediation service that still facilitates numerous out-of-court, less expensive, and less confrontational settlements between parties. The *Oklahoma Conference of Churches* established a hot-line in their own office and then worked very closely with their state's governor and the Department of Mental Health, as well as with a group of concerned farm and community organizations to put in place an exemplary suicide prevention program. In *Wyoming*, a skilled and committed laywoman enlisted the support of the faith community, every farm organization in the state, and the state's community colleges, Extension Service, and mental health center in a coordinated and effective response to the crisis. In some states, including *Missouri*, Jewish groups actively worked with the Christian community to raise awareness of the hate groups that were working among desperate farmers to blame Jews and other groups for the crisis and then to sell farmers illegal and counterproductive "solutions" for paying off their debts.

5. A related historical issue that we will not elaborate in this volume is the story of the sharecropping families, both black and white, who were forced off the land and into urban centers by changes in technology and cropping systems, primarily in the South. While many found the resources to transform their lives of grinding poverty into opportunity and upward socioeconomic mobility, many others have never been able to gain an economic foothold in the urban economy. It can be argued that this story is another example of the consequences of a past rural crisis contributing to a present urban one.

6. This study was conducted by William D. Heffernan, Judith Bortner Heffernan, and Christine Hard of the University of Missouri in the spring of 1990.

7. An excellent and concise discussion of many aspects of this topic is Osha Gray Davidson's book *Broken Heartland: The Rise of America's Rural Ghetto* (New York: Doubleday, 1990).

8. It must be noted that the profound change that we will discuss here in the context of rural America is one that is transforming virtually every sector of the *global* economy. To assist in understanding the impact of this change on rural America and the families, institutions, and communities therein, we will focus here on what is happening in the agricultural or food system sector of the economy.

9. The term, "transnational corporation," commonly refers to firms that locate their headquarters in one country, produce products in other, usually low wages countries, and then sell the products in still other countries. Two excellent sources of information on this topic are the book by Professor Alessandro Bonanno et. al, entitled *From Columbus to ConAgra: The Globalization of Agriculture and Food* (Lawrence, Kansas: University of Kansas Press, 1994), and the numerous articles by Professor William D. Heffernan who has documented these changes for over twenty-five years.

10. See, e.g., Dale Kasler, "Iowa Manufacturing Sees a Rural Re-birth," *Des Moines Register*, February 18 1996, 1A.

11. "Rural Development," *1995 Farm Bill—Guidance of the Administration* (U.S. Department of Agriculture: Rural Economic & Community Development, 1996), 7.

12. Kenneth M. Johnson and Calvin L. Beale, "The Rural Rebound Revisited," *American Demographics* 17:7 (July 1995), 46, 48.

13. Ibid, 46.

14. "Nonmetro Population Continues Past-1990 Rebound," *Rural Conditions and Trends* (Washington D.C.: USDA Economic Research Service, Spring 1995), 6.

15. Johnson and Beale, "The Rural Rebound Revisited," 48.

16. The statistics in the last two paragraphs are drawn from Johnson and Beale, "The Rural Rebound Revisited," 46-54.

17. *Statistical Abstracts of the United States* 1978, 1995.

18. See Walter Goldschmidt, *As You Sow: Three Studies in the Social Consequences of Agribusiness* (Montclair, N.J.: Allanheld, Osmun & Co., 1978). Reviewing the results of similar studies Dean MacCannell reaches the same conclusion; Dean MacCannell, "Agribusiness and the Small Community" master's thesis, University of California-Davis, n.d. See also Marty Strange, *Family Farming: A New Economic Vision* (Lincoln: University of Nebraska Press; and San Francisco: Institute for Food and Development Policy, 1988), especially pp. 52–55 and 85–100.

19. These changes were identified by Dr. Janet M. Fitchen, Professor of Anthropology at Ithaca College, Ithaca, New York. A widely recognized authority on rural poverty, Janet's work was supported by grants from the National Institute for Mental Health and the Ford Foundation. She is the author of *Poverty in Rural America* (Boulder: Westview, 1981), and *Endangered Spaces, Endearing Places: Change, Identity and Survival in Rural America* (Boulder: Westview, 1991).

20. For examples of ways that environmental concerns and economic ones can be approached simultaneously, see Bill McKibben, *Hope Human and Wild: True Stories of Living Lightly on the Earth* (Boston: Little, Brown, 1995). See also Keith Schneider, "For the Environment, Compassion Fatigue," *The New York Times*, November 6, 1994, E3. On the rural, and smaller member church's role in promoting concern for

creation, see Shannon Jung, "Grounded in God: Ecology, Consumption, and the Small Church," *Anglican Theological Review*, Fall 1996.

Chapter 6

1. Tex Sample, *Ministry in an Oral Culture: Living with Will Rogers, Uncle Remus, and Minnie Pearl* (Louisville: Westminster/John Knox, 1994).

2. Gallup Poll, reported in *Christian Century*, June 29-July 6, 1994, 636.

3. While it would be convenient to settle on one image of the church in rural America that captured all that the church is and all the theology it incorporates, that is not possible or desirable. Let us then offer a number of images that are appropriate to this context. The church can be seen as the "family of God," the "body of Christ" or the "embodied Christ"; others suggest that the rural church be seen as the "servant church."

Yet others would want to emphasize different aspects of the church: the fact that in church people find those who care for one another; that we are connected through the church to all other Christians; that we are a covenanted community; that we are the keepers of the garden. All these images and tasks are clearly Bible-based.

4. Gary P. Burkart and David C. Lege, *Parish Life in Town and Countryside*, Notre Dame Study of Catholic Parish Life no. 13 (1988), 9.

5. J. Paul Rajashekar and Götz Planer-Friedrich, eds., *Land Is Life: Toward a Just Sharing of Land*, LWF Documentation 27 (Geneva: Lutheran World Federation, 1990).

6. Rural communities resist homogenization. The tendency of modernity is to replace one culture by another, the latter usually under the control of those outside the original culture. We do not want television to define the limits of acceptable behavior or to mandate casual sex or obnoxious boorishness or violence for its adolescent and pre-adolescent viewers. Such universalizing agents tend to make rural people feel disadvantaged and unfashionable ("out of it"); we do not think they appreciate the values of family and mutuality and character that we do.

7. Walter Brueggemann, *Texts Under Negotiation: The Bible and Postmodern Imagination* (Minneapolis: Fortress, 1993), 35.

8. Allen Bloom, *Love and Friendship*, quoted by William Cash, "Fallen Angels," *South China Sunday Morning Post Magazine*, October 3, 1993, 10.

9. Douglas Alan Walrath, "The Hazards of Globalism," *Viewpoints*, Occasional Essays by Faculty at Bangor Theological Seminary, Bangor, Maine, October 1991, no pagination.

10. Tony Pappas, *Mustard Seeds: Devotions for Small Church People* (Columbus, Ga.: Brentwood Christian Press, 1994), 67–68, and Shannon

Jung, "A Place From Which to Relate: Land, Ethnicity, and Nationhood," *The Annual of the Society of Christian Ethics, 1994.*

11. Dorothee Soelle, *Theology for Skeptics: Reflections on God* (Minneapolis: Fortress, 1995), 72.

12. Jean Vanier, *From Brokenness to Community* (Mahwah, N.J.: Paulist, 1991), 20–21.

13. Ibid., 21–22.

Chapter 7

1. An early challenge setting forth the need to move onto a sustainable path of development is Lester R. Brown, *Building a Sustainable Society* (New York: Norton, 1981).

2. The need for a new concept of economic welfare, including the health of the environment and conservation of natural resources, is excellently articulated in Herman E. Daly and John B. Cobb, *For the Common Good: Redirecting the Economy Toward Community, the Environment, and a Sustainable Future* (Boston: Beacon, 1989).

3. World Commission on Environment and Development, *Our Common Future* (New York: Oxford University Press, 1987), 47.

4. See Lester R. Brown, Hal Kane, and Ed Ayres, *Vital Signs 1994* (New York: Norton, 1994), 15–20.

5. Ibid., 15.

6. See Richard Cartwright Austin, "The Spiritual Crisis of Modern Agriculture," *Christian Social Action* 7 (October 1994), 4–11.

7. David Ostendorf, "Work Harder for Rural-Urban Links," *Des Moines Register*, July 26, 1994.

8. Barbara Ward and Rene Dubos, *Only One Earth: The Care and Maintenance of a Small Planet* (New York: Norton, 1972), 12.

9. For a comprehensive view of recent accomplishments by United Nations agencies as they form a global partnership of action in addressing environmental issues, see Hillary F. French, "Forging a New Global Partnership," in Lester R. Brown and others, *State of the World 1995* (New York: Norton, 1995), 170–89.

10. Thomas Berry, *The Dream of the Earth* (San Francisco: Sierra Club Books, 1988), xiii.

11. Al Gore in *Earth in the Balance: Ecology and the Human Spirit* (Boston: Houghton Mifflin, 1992), 269, identifies five inhibitors that threaten planetary survival: individual rights independent of a sense of obligation; the pervasiveness of corruption that inhibits a healthy sense of ecological accountability; widespread tolerance of injustice; third world development needs seen as short-term meeting of basic necessities rather than addressing long-term concerns; and the need for a better understanding of development in the thinking of the Western world.

12. For a study of the need for the preservation of the health of the land in relation to the question of long-ranging perspectives on the

capacity of the nation to produce food, see Freudenberger, *Food for Tomorrow?* (Minneapolis: Augsburg, 1984).

13. Lester R. Brown, "Who Will Feed China?" *World Watch,* September/October 1994, 10–19.

14. A working understanding of "significant prophetic voice" can be seen in the reading of Walter Brueggemann, *The Prophetic Imagination* (Philadelphia: Fortress, 1978).

Chapter 8

1. Jim Wallis, *The Soul of Politics: Beyond "Religious Right" and "Secular Left"* (New York: Harcourt, Brace & Co., 1995), 85.

2. Ibid., 27.

3. Ibid., 45.

4. Michael J. Schultheis, Edward P. De Berri, and Peter J. Henriot, *Our Best Kept Secret: The Rich Heritage of Catholic Social Teaching* (Washington, D.C.: Center of Concern, 1987).

5. Boniface Ramsey, *Beginning to Read the Fathers* (New York: Paulist, 1985), 14.

6. Deborah K. Cronin, *The NOW (rm) Strategy Workbook* (Produced by General Board of Global Ministries, National Division, The United Methodist Church, 1994).

7. Walter Burghardt, S.J., "Characteristics of Social Justice Spirituality," *Origins* 24 (July 1994), 163–64.

8. Dorothee Soelle, *Theology for Skeptics: Reflections on God* (Minneapolis: Fortress, 1995), 16.

9. Wallis, *The Soul of Politics*, p.53.

Chapter 9

1. Robert Coles, *Children of Crisis,* Volume 2: *Migrants, Sharecroppers and Mountaineers* (New York: Little, Brown, 1973).

2. Robert A. Caro, *The Path to Power* (New York: Random House, 1990).

3. The preceding two pages are heavily indebted to Brother David Andrews, C.S.C., Esq., Executive Director, National Catholic Rural Life Conference.

4. The Most Reverend Victor H. Balke, Catholic Bishop of the Crookston, Minnesota, diocese.

5. The Reverend Ed Kail, a United Methodist pastor and professor at the Saint Paul School of Theology, Kansas City, contributed a great deal to this section on the role of rural pastors.

6. Sensitivity to diverse groups who may not share Christian beliefs is in keeping with the high value our faith places on hospitality.

7. See Deborah Cronin, *Can Your Dog Hunt?* (Lima, Ohio: Fairway Press, 1995). This whole section has benefitted from District Superintendent Cronin's insights in that book.

8. For the full report, see Shannon Jung and Kris Kirst, "Revitalization in the Rural Congregation: What We Know, What We Need to Know," Studies in Rural Ministry II, An Occasional Series, Center for Theology and Land, 2000 University Avenue, Dubuque, IA 52001.

9. There is a growing literature that, not surprisingly, comes from the Alban Institute's leadership: Celia Hahn, *Growing in Authority, Relinquishing Control* (Washington D.C.: Alban Institute, 1995); Stevens and Collins, *Equipping the Pastor: A Systems Approach to Congregational Leadership* (Washington D.C.: Alban Institute, 1992); and Stewart Zabriskie, *Total Ministry* (Washington D.C.: Alban Institute, 1995).

10. See Shannon Jung and Mary Agria, *Rural Congregational Studies: A Guide for Good Shepherds* (Nashville: Abingdon, 1997).

INDEX

CMS (Church Membership Survey), 58

coalition, 32, 33, 175, 182, 186, 219

Coles, Robert, 195, 243

collaboration, 9, 185-86

Colonial Period, 37-38

common good, 27, 136

community, 10, 16, 17, 18, 19, 21, 22, 23, 26, 27, 28, 29, 30, 31, 33, 34, 62, 64, 67, 72, 89, 102, 103, 106, 111, 113, 128, 130-33, 136, 140, 141, 146, 147, 151, 155, 158, 165, 167, 172, 179, 180-83, 186, 189, 192, 193, 197, 203, 211-12, 215, 218, 226-28

community organizing, 216-17

community service trends, 111-16, 199, 203, 210

confession, 121, 147, 148

conflict, 63, 118, 131, 151, 182, 212

congregation, 11, 12, 20, 28, 29, 72, 76, 77, 82, 94, 100, 120, 137, 141-42, 150, 163, 173, 176, 186, 189, 190, 195, 199, 208, 215, 218, 221

Congregationalists, 39

consolidation, 46, 47

contextualization, 49, 50, 63, 195, 220

continuing education, 210, 213-14

cooperative churches, 47, 52, 122, 186-87

corporate policies, 20, 29, 56, 103, 105, 107-111, 152, 184, 220

Country Life Movement, 42-49

covenant, 14, 165

creation, 14, 18, 20, 22, 23, 54, 119, 128, 136, 139, 140, 155, 165, 182, 193

crisis, 10, 16, 17, 55, 114, 153, 158, 166

Cronin, Deborah, 197, 204, 205, 231, 242, 243

CSA (Congregation/Community Supported Agriculture), 34

culture, 30, 58, 118, 136-37, 138, 149, 175, 194, 195, 196

Cushman, Jim, 13

Daugherty, Mary Lee, 13

decline, 20, 21, 23, 25, 28, 120, 124, 126, 135, 143, 145, 188-89, 190

democratic society, 18, 113

denominations, 9, 26, 28, 29, 34, 43, 47, 49, 52, 59, 60, 61, 63, 69, 71, 72, 77, 82, 122, 145, 174, 192, 213, 218, 219

Department of Church and Country Life, 44

development, 117, 118, 120, 188, 189, 190, 192, 198, 220

dignity of the person, 165, 167, 168

disciple, 172, 173, 208

Disciples of Christ, 67, 71

DuBois, W. E. B., 45, 236

Dubos, Rene, 158, 159, 242

Dudley, Carl, 79, 94, 237

ecclesiological ecology, 77, 81, 174, 175, 177

economy, 27, 28, 29, 32, 97, 98, 99, 102-103, 106, 110, 111-14, 118, 119, 143, 149, 158, 160, 162, 184, 191, 215, 226

ecumenical shared ministries, 34, 187, 204

ecumenicity, 9, 132, 175, 177, 186

electronic media, 64, 208, 214, 229-30